Undefeated

MARSHA HUNT

UNDEFEATED

MAINSTREAM
PUBLISHING

EDINBURGH AND LONDON

First published in Great Britain in 2005 by
MAINSTREAM PUBLISHING COMPANY
(EDINBURGH) LTD
7 Albany Street
Edinburgh EH1 3UG

ISBN 1 84596 078 5

A catalogue record for this book is available
from the British Library

Typeset in Caslon, Goudy Sans and Zapf Chancery

Printed in Great Britain by
Cox & Wyman Ltd

*Ten per cent of the royalties for this book will go to ARC Cancer
Support Centre, Dublin (Registered Charity No. CHY 1085)*

For
the silver man,
with whom I danced

Contents

The End?

Maybe I'll be dead by the time you read this. Maybe not. But should breast cancer be credited with ending my life, know this: cancer didn't kill me. I died for a cause.

After I discovered that I'd personally witnessed an extraordinary piece of history, for the sake of lodging my testimony, I was willing to give my life – so that somebody would know, at least from my point of view, how my generation got lost. What didn't register with me in the summer of 2004 when that lump started growing in my breast is that cancer was becoming as much a part of our slot in history as rock and roll, the Pill, sex and TV.

I've done a lot of travelling. Made a bunch of trips in my time. But at this junction, I'd say my cancer trip is amongst the most rewarding. As Friedrich Nietzsche said, 'That which does not kill us makes us stronger.' Inspiring quotations like his helped fuel me for this journey, so I'll share some with you, while I share my crazy cancer story.

I

Against the Ropes

*If a man hasn't discovered something
he will die for, he isn't fit to live.*

MARTIN LUTHER KING

1

Jimi Hendrix and Me

When I decided to risk my life for Jimi Hendrix, he'd been dead for 34 years. Dead since 1970 when I'd had my last hit single, I was Mick Jagger's brown sugar and had Mick's baby. That baby's now 34, and her being pregnant with her second child had everything to do with how I recently played my hand when I got the bad news.

Looking back, I guess anybody would view what I did as suicidal. But by my reckoning, I was doing what was right, what had to be done. The fact that my life depended upon it seemed irrelevant. I was sure that since I alone had witnessed something that the world needed to know about, I had a duty to report it at whatever cost to myself, because it alters our sense of modern history. As a writer, that seemed worth dying for.

There I was, tucked away in northern France in my craggy little writing studio, speaking to virtually no one. Every day, I'd rise early to take an hour's walk out of the village, up the steep hill and into the wide open countryside. It was late spring, early

June, so everything was very green and still growing at a rapid rate. The local farmers had corn, wheat and sugar beet pushing up so fast you could practically hear them growing either side of the road. Seeing that growth each morning affected me, because I related it to my writing. Words sprouted on the page and the pages mounted each day.

But it was an unexpected meeting with Mick's writing partner, Keith Richards, for the first time on 6 June 2004, which inspired me to tell Jimi's story in a more personal way, beginning with meeting Keith that day. It had been my theory that Jimi's rock career, launched in Britain in the autumn of '66 was intriguingly dependent upon Keith to such an extent that, had it not been for Keith, Jimi wouldn't have become the first black rock star. Meeting Keith at Mick's French chateau provided me with a new angle from which to approach Jimi's story.

It happened to be the 60th anniversary of the Allies' D-Day invasion. That it was coincidentally Mother's Day in France made the afternoon seem all the more auspicious. I'd driven down to Mick's to show him the diamond earrings that he'd recently sent me. Keith was there to write songs, and everything about that providential meeting told me to scrap what I'd been writing for four and a half years and start over.

That I was meeting Keith for the first time was bizarre considering that I'd known Mick since 1969. I had intentionally avoided him because his notorious addiction and reputed interest in the occult made him a no-go area for me.

When Keith turned to me during lunch and said, 'We're connected. You know that, don't you?' I was tempted to say, 'You don't know how much!' He was fun, and when he told Mick, 'I'm gonna get this girl singing,' I really laughed. But as much as I was enjoying that afternoon in the sun, when Keith said, 'Stay,' I made a feeble excuse about why I had to leave immediately after lunch. I could barely wait to high tail it back to my studio and start the rewrite sparked by meeting him.

Before I go any further, it's important for you to know that I was really broke, and had it not been for my overdraft at the Allied Irish Bank, all the time that I spent researching and writing about Jimi never could have happened. I'd been working on that book for years without any pay but still flying hither, thither and yonder for research as though I was living on an advance. I was writing without a commission and had reached that point in penury when I avoided putting petrol in the car until I suspected it was almost bone dry. But understand that, for me, being broke has nothing to do with being poor or feeling poor.

Money has never been a priority; it's not what I strive for nor ever have. Yet by some miracle, for the sake of Jimi's story I've managed to get to where I've had to be. Intermittently that was my writing studio, called '*la montagne*'. The English would call it a cottage. It seems to be the only place that I can write. It's my hideaway, tucked out of the way in a tiny rural village about 90 miles due north of Paris.

So there you have the picture . . . It's maybe mid-June; I'm in France, broke and, thanks to meeting Keith Richards at Mick's, I'm into a complete rewrite on a book about Jimi that I've been working on exclusively for four and half years. My thirty-three-year-old daughter and only child, Karis Jagger, is pregnant in LA and due to visit me in France for a week in early August with her three-year-old daughter, Mazie.

Basically, all seemed well with the world. Then I slipped into bed one night, exhausted after a day's writing, to discover that, on rolling over onto my stomach to sleep, there was a slight tenderness in my right breast. I was neither alarmed nor particularly interested and thought maybe I'd bumped it at some point and hadn't noticed. As I recall, I gave my breast a couple of prods in the dark. Didn't even bother switching the light on to check before turning over on my side and forgetting about it. I mention it because now everybody – doctors, nurses, friends – they all want me to pinpoint when I first noticed that there was a problem.

For as long as I can remember, I'd had a lump the size of an olive in my right breast. During a routine health check when I was an 18-year-old freshman at UC Berkeley, the university hospital suggested that I have the lump removed even though it was benign. I refused their offer and was glad because, years later, it was diagnosed as a swollen gland. I thought no good would come from sticking needles in it each year for a biopsy and so I didn't.

My breasts have played a unique role in my life. Displaying them for the camera began at university in 1964, this being the year when we Berkeley students were sitting in for the Free Speech Movement, smoking pot, experimenting with acid, lining up to take oriental philosophy courses, daring to co-habit and going to dances in San Francisco. An art photographer, Bill Piltzer, was highly regarded around campus, so I was chuffed that he thought me worthy to be one of his black-and-white nature studies, along with leaves and trees and others such things he shot. Nudity in art photography was as respectable as nudes painted on canvas, and Bill had me posing for shots in which my nakedness was merely implied.

Though nudity at that point had yet to become a statement about liberation, 18 months later in February of '66 when I arrived in London, things were rapidly moving in that direction. London was suddenly at the forefront of everything from fashion and photography to music. It was miniskirt headquarters. The unexpected emergence of the working class pushed everything to the outer limits and suddenly it was good to have an accent from the East End or the bowels of Birmingham. Among the list of working-class heroes were Mary Quant, Vidal Sassoon, David Bailey, Terence Stamp and Ken Loach. And there I was in London, this Negro kid from Berkeley, when Berkeley was *the* college town at the vanguard of the student movement, with neighbouring San Francisco about to hit its own zenith, and, since Motown was the sound of the day, anybody looking and talking vaguely like a Supreme was considered gorgeous.

Six thousand miles from my mother's interference, I was up for almost anything just as the Pill, English rock and roll and the working class burst onto the scene. Close on their heels was the mushrooming drug culture. Oddly, though I looked the part, I didn't touch drugs for fear of being deported if arrested.

Suddenly bold girls were baring their breasts and nudity was fashion. Models wearing only make-up and a coy expression were considered daring but acceptable. And there was I, with my colour and nationality playing a crucial role, just as the Jimi Hendrix Experience took Britain by storm in the late autumn of '66. With their lookalike nappy hair, and Jimi injecting English rock with his American Negro R&B licks and struts and sexuality, that little trio turned London upside down and made being an American Negro in town a major calling card, but they also made Motown look and sound passé. This unique mix of a Negro guy and two whites put to rest some sexual taboos about our race. Up to that point, we were untouchables.

What did this have to do with my breasts then and now?

Just about everything.

Black is Beautiful had yet to happen. Believe it or not, the English, thinking they were being polite, still called us coloured. But within a couple of months of that trio making its debut on TV and radio, looking like Jimi was in. It was a time when London was all about fashion and image. It opened doors for us in London, us being young American Negroes. We numbered about ten.

It was 1967, and it was impossible not to be advantaged by the circumstances . . . It cast an undue glow upon me, young, independent and free wheeling as I was.

Of course, I now see all this with the benefit of both hindsight and my recent years of research on how the Jimi Hendrix Experience sparked social changes. Now I can see without question that getting my first job singing in a London blues band probably had a great deal to do with the Jimi Hendrix Experience having their first single, 'Hey Joe', topping the English charts at the time and Jimi, with his unruly naps, emerging as the new sex symbol. At the time, it wasn't apparent that I was destined to walk in his shadow but leave my own tracks.

In London, notions and expectations about black sexuality were heightened by Jimi's promotion as leader of the Jimi Hendrix Experience. I'd argue that this had nothing to do with me personally, yet it had a lot to do with the attention I got and the opportunities that came my way. Sex and race. Race and sex. The way the two have remained powerfully linked through American slavery is something that people are still unwilling to address. For me, young and London-based, I was oblivious to how much of a role the colour of my skin was playing in what was happening to me on a daily basis.

In 1968, I got a small part in *Hair*, the first rock musical, which had been the hit of the season on Broadway. When it opened in London with an English cast and a few of us Americans, the show-stopping number that I sang lead on was a spoof on the Supremes, and in a white platinum wig, I sang a song about how delicious white boys were. 'White boys give me goosebumps, white boys give me chills,' so the lyrics began. But what really caused all the hubbub was our cast of 26 appearing naked in a dim blue light just as the curtain came down on the first act. It was supposed to be an act of liberation, but the media seemed to miss the point. The element of titillation probably helped sell seats, but it aggravated me that they didn't get it, and I rarely stripped after the first night.

The day after we opened to rave front-page notices was a Thursday – 26 September, I think. I turned up at the theatre early like the rest of the cast to get notes, and the show's very haughty publicist, Wendy Hanson, took me aside to ask if I'd do a nude photo session with Patrick, the Earl of Lichfield, for American *Vogue*. He's Queen Elizabeth's cousin and was this very handsome bachelor about town, best known for his photos of the Royal Family. So I laughed. I've got two lines in a show that all of London's talking about and Lichfield and *Vogue* want me? My breasts weren't all that great. Also, pin-thin thighs were the fashion and mine resembled those of a rugby player. However, black models almost never appeared in American *Vogue* back then, so I considered the assignment a challenge and turned up early with my make-up and false lashes, and combed my hair out as big as I could get it. It was a much bigger version of Noel Redding's, the bass player in the Jimi Hendrix Experience.

After that Lichfield session, my breasts got a lot of public airing. Nudity was in, and I saw it as positive, an advance on the old mores and a rejection of sexual repression. Why be embarrassed about your body? I considered it one of my human rights to bare mine and did. Whether it was the cartoonist Ralph Steadman painting a royal crest upon my breasts for the *Sunday Telegraph*, or David Bailey photographing me nude for the sleeve of my first single, or appearing as a bare-breasted vampire in a horror movie, I exposed my body without shame. I even believed that, as a rock artist, having been signed in April 1969 by the same small London label that had launched the Jimi Hendrix Experience, I was helping to erase racial taboos, particularly sexual ones, in Britain and Europe as Jimi was continuing to do worldwide. We were no longer untouchables. We'd become the 'in' thing.

I've never understood why one particular shot from Lichfield's session has continued to appear in newspapers, magazines and promotional material throughout the course of the past 37 years. It was recently part of his exhibition at the National Portrait Gallery and graces the cover of this book. But by posing for Lichfield and appearing naked in newspapers and magazines, on TV and film, had I unwittingly promoted the false notion that a female's sexuality is determined by her two breasts? Had I planted seeds that would produce a poison flower?

In 2004, long after I had given up singing, let alone posing nude, that question was going to be answered for me in ways I hadn't bargained for. By then, I didn't have a real man in my life. Nor was I looking for one. Jimi was my obsession, yet I have always resisted being anybody's fan. I appreciated his talent, but in truth I wasn't that interested in his music until January 2000, when I told my ex-literary agent, David Godwin, that I was never going to write another book.

'You were born to write Hendrix's biography,' were David's words. Many years earlier, I had suggested writing Jimi's biography but had forgotten all about it. David seemed so certain that I felt challenged to find out if he was right. Discovering on the Internet that 13 biographies had been written in English alone could have put me off, but I decided to make Noel Redding the litmus test. He'd been the bass player with the Jimi Hendrix Experience from 1966 to '69. As one of the trio, I figured he'd have as true a picture of the band and Jimi during their meteoric rise as anybody living.

There were a couple of good omens. Not only had Noel settled in 1975 on Ireland's south coast, just west of Clonakilty, I'd also heard that Steve Housden, an Australian guitarist, occasionally played with him in a pub band that did local gigs. Steve had been in my band when I was living in Sydney in 1981 but left me to join the Little River Band. He'd been with them ever since. Tracking down his number in Clonakilty was the beginning of my journey into a heart of darkness. Noel's revelations about Jimi had everything to do with my determination to expose Jimi's sad story, and he became my star witness, the person I would call to check details as I went in search of the facts.

The Jimi Hendrix Experience had released four albums, all of which included Noel on bass, so I expected him to be living like rock royalty, but he'd been receiving no royalties, and his damp, rambling house with its leaky roof was testimony to that. With Noel's initial help, I not only began to research Jimi's life but Noel and I, and his American girlfriend, Deborah McNaughton, who lived with him, began a friendship that became increasingly important to me.

In 2001, when Deborah got breast cancer, her decision to return to Santa Fe for treatment meant that Noel, with his drinking problem, was left to cope on his own. A call from Deborah in New Mexico to Steve Housden's wife, June, to check on Noel, led to June finding Noel's body at home. His death in May 2002 contributed to my commitment to paint a true picture of the Jimi Hendrix Experience and the social as well as musical contributions that Jimi, Noel and their drummer, Mitch Mitchell, had made.

Research and writing was a complicated process. Since heroin and prostitution were involved in the story, it took time to get people to talk. And, as with my meeting with Keith in 2004, one person's testimony could force me to reconsider my whole approach to the story. As the facts mounted, I discovered that I was a major witness to Jimi's life and times and it was my duty to rewrite his place in history. 'Write on!' my will insisted two years after Noel's death. 'Write on!' it wailed after meeting Keith Richards at Mick's in June.

The tender spot in my breast made me give up sleeping on my stomach by August, and I made a point of not mentioning it to my daughter, Karis, who was five months pregnant when she came to visit me in France with three-year-old Mazie.

The lump grew larger in September and by mid-October, when I flew to New York in the hope of tracking down a Trinidadian friend of Jimi's who was in his early 70s with severe health problems, I'd convinced myself that, although I was putting my own health at risk, any interruptions in my writing at that stage could make me lose my focus on the picture that had been gradually unveiling itself before me since 2000.

Researching Jimi's history had exposed a unique picture of our race, our generation and the way in which Atlantic crossings between British and American bands had confused and killed the political promise of the '60s. Having walked in his shadow, I came to believe what David Godwin had told me, which is that I was born to write this story.

But whether I was bathing or dressing, there was no forgetting that something was wrong and had been for months with my right breast. By late October, I was telling friends and rang my homoeopath in Ireland, who had recommended a remedy to reduce the swelling.

A book for a life? Was it a rational exchange?

Sometimes the truth is worth dying for.

*You must do that thing
you think you cannot do.*

ELEANOR ROOSEVELT

2

Dr Feelgood

I know that it's ridiculous to judge a man by his shoes. Unless he's wearing suede Hush Puppies, that is. So I always check. Mr Arnold Hill was wearing black loafers. They weren't exactly scuffed but nor were they polished. I was eyeing them as I followed him into his office at St Vincent's Private Hospital. I was alone. So was he. There was no nurse. His secretary remained seated in the outer office.

I had worn a black, loose-fitting, short-sleeved top that was easy to remove, because I knew he'd ask me to take it off, but, before he did, he sat at his desk and asked me a load of other questions. He had that Irish accent that always stops me in my tracks. Hearing his dis for this and dat for that reminded me that the English that slaves learned came from Ireland. Not that I was sure he was pure Irish. His hair was black, his slim face slightly sallow, his features sharp. But that accent was distinctly Irish, and I felt immediately comfortable with him after he reached over to shake my hand and said, 'I'm Arnie Hill.'

I guessed him to be in his mid to late 30s, and I knew before I accepted the lunch-time appointment that he was top notch and had accepted me as a client because I came recommended by another young Dublin surgeon, Majella Doyle, the daughter of my homoeopath, Marie Doyle.

As a child, I'd loved that my father was a doctor, a psychiatrist, yet I'm now wary of doctors and their pills, and avoid both whenever I can. But by 16 November 2004, my right breast was so sore and the lump had become so large that I'd given up taking the homoeopathic medicine that was meant to reduce the swelling.

Arnie Hill opened a folder on which my name was jotted. I could see it from where I was seated opposite him. Was this going to be my lucky day, when I finally heard from a specialist that there was nothing to worry about because the swelling in my breast was a gland gone mad? I wasn't exactly banking on it, but I still felt that I had a 50–50 chance.

Should I have had a mammogram taken while I was in New York? Had I been wise to wait until I got back to Ireland? I thought so. In New York, I would have been a number. In Ireland, I was a name, respected as a writer, with a host of friends that I knew I could depend upon if worst ever came to worst. I also had experience of dealing with the medical profession here because my ex-partner, Alan Gilsenan, had been diagnosed with cancer at St Vincent's Teaching Hospital and treated at the Mater Private. Unlike him, I had no partner, would have no advocate, nobody watching my back. Since our split in 2000, I'd been celibate.

Having worked on Jimi's story since then, being alone suited me. I could hop on a plane to go interview somebody, as I'd recently done in New York, and stay as long as was necessary without guilt or apology. I need a sense of detachment to write.

I can't seem to concentrate if my diary's full of expectations. Just knowing that I have a dinner appointment can screw up my writing day. Even a phone call or the arrival of a repairman can make me lose my focus until I find that total silence again that frees my mind and lets me spread my thoughts out like so many pieces of a jigsaw puzzle waiting to be fitted together. Aloneness suits me, and it's made me adept at fighting my corner and watching my own back. I wasn't in the least afraid of coming to this crucial appointment alone.

Arnie Hill was sitting with his back to a window that overlooked the hospital's car park, and while he asked the rote questions about my general health, my mind drifted back to 1996, when I'd driven Alan to this hospital for a bowel check-up and spotted a friend of his mother's walking past. It was her narrow ankles of all things that I had recognised from behind, and I leapt out of the car to call her name.

'Kitty, is that you?'

I'd only been with her and her sister, Yvonne Fitzgerald, what seemed like a week before. At the time, they were getting ready to go to the hairdresser's, and we sat in Yvonne's living room finishing our tea while she talked about selling her enormous house, which was located in Sandymount, one of the nicest of the residential areas of central Dublin. They'd both been for mammograms, and it turned out that they both had tumours. Kitty's was more serious than Yvonne's, and I didn't realise that she had become a patient at St Vincent's.

'Can you believe it?' I laughed when she turned in the car park to see who'd called. 'I recognised you from behind by your ankles!'

I knew that she would recognise me from that distance of 50 yards because I had my hair down and there were virtually no black faces in Dublin in '96.

'Hello,' she called as she approached. 'What are you doing here?'

'Waiting for Alan. He's seeing a specialist.'

The Irish are clannish, and the island is small. With a population of three and half million, it seems that everybody is somehow related to everybody else. The nuclear families are large, especially the older generations. It was nothing to meet one of Alan's mother's friends who was born in the 1930s and grew up in a family of ten kids. So it's to be expected that everybody knows everybody and it's not easy to keep your business to yourself. I knew that word would spread that Kitty had seen me and that Alan was having a check-up at the hospital. Not that it mattered. What mattered was that Kitty had breast cancer.

I promised to visit her the next day and did. She talked about wanting to write, and I advised her on how to go about it and eventually sent her a blank notepad and pencils with a letter saying, 'Go to it.'

She really wanted to. But time marched on and maybe her illness got in the way. It troubled me the following year when I heard that she'd died. Her sister, Yvonne, managed to sell the house for a fortune, and while she was waiting to buy something else, my ex-stepfather came to visit me and the dinner she invited him to was one of the highlights of his trip. So it troubled me even more hearing from Alan that Yvonne had also died of breast cancer while I was gallivanting about the world piecing together the facts about Jimi.

These memories reeled through my head while Arnie Hill's pen scribbled down the answers to his standard queries.

'I first noticed some tenderness in my breast in June, but I'd had the swollen gland in my breast for so long that I assumed that it was playing up.'

He had an easy manner, albeit detached. I sensed that he was a very busy young surgeon managing not to seem rushed. It would be too much to say his face was kind, but it hedged just close enough to handsome to appeal to me.

How many breasts had he seen that day, I wondered, as I exposed mine, saying, 'Well, if you're a breast man, you've picked the right job.' Unfortunately, I find I say the damnedest things when I'm in an embarrassing situation, and, for some reason, as he reached to feel the lump in my right breast, I felt this was one.

As he probed, I was studying his eyes, looking for his prognosis before he uttered one. He was wearing a grey suit. Well cut. Possibly Italian. The cuff of his shirt peered from his sleeve as I watched his white hand prod my brown breast.

'What d'you think?' I asked casually, thinking that whatever he thought, I'd soon be out of there, and he'd be on to his next appointment. But it was his air of professional proficiency that took me off guard when he said in one breath, 'I think this is cancer.'

I couldn't believe he said it. Does cancer have a feel? I was sitting up topless, with my legs dangling off the side of the gurney, and I looked down at my right breast. Cancer? Naw. Really? Cancer? I wanted to roll the word around in my mouth, because it seemed quite silly that it could apply to me. But what had been merely a swelling now seemed to have a hard edge.

The room was quiet as I slipped my bra back on. Then my shirt.

'I'll be damned.' I was thinking. 'Fucking cancer.'

'You'll need a mammogram, and if that's not clear, you'll have an ultrasound, and if that's not clear, you'll have a biopsy.'

'All today? You mean like right away?'

'Yes,' he said, picking up the phone.

'Well, sister,' I was still having a private conversation in my head. 'Just as well you brought your ass to Ireland, cause it would never happen this way in New York. Getting results from the mammogram alone would have taken weeks.' While struggling with my bra clasp, I was thinking, 'Thank God for fucking Ireland.'

Swearing takes the edge off things. I enjoy it, and when you get bad news, that's the time to do anything that will allow you a bit of enjoyment.

I felt safe. It was a strange thing to note under the circumstances. I wasn't a bit worried. Everything about him, the small hospital, its connection to the public hospital and the fact that it had a special breast-care building told me that this situation was as good as it gets. Most of the doctors, surgeons and specialists working at St Vincent's Private Hospital also serve the large public hospital to which it's attached, and now there's a spanking new breast-care centre located between the two. That it's the largest and most up to date in Ireland gave me the feeling that if I had to be any place with breast cancer, this was the place to be. But I had a few shocks waiting for me.

When I took the chair opposite him again, having slipped my top on, I examined him with different eyes. I didn't care what kind of shoes he wore. The cut of his suit was irrelevant, and I no longer saw him as a boy. Here was a man who might have to take a scalpel to me.

'I'd like you to come back on Friday,' he said. 'Can you do that?'

'Absolutely. And if this is cancer, will you be my doctor?'

'Yes,' he smiled, handing me a piece of paper.

'Take dis. Speak to my secretary. She'll set up Friday's appointment.'

The glass that I had to press my breast upon on the mammogram machine was cold. The female technician operating it apologised. 'This will feel uncomfortable,' she said, 'but it doesn't take long.'

I winced and held my breath when the machine squeezed my right breast hard. It had become so tender that the slightest touch hurt. So I gritted my teeth and said fuck under my breath. Thankfully, the screening of the left breast didn't hurt half as much, and I was congratulating myself for wearing the easy-to-remove top when the technician told me to take the X-rays she'd produced down to Ultrasound.

Whoops . . . she's not saying all clear go home . . .

'It's just past the reception area,' she said.

Her voice sounded distant, because a touch of jet lag was hitting me by then. Not so much that I had to immediately find a place to put my head down, which can sometimes be the case, but my mind had became a little fuzzy, and my hearing felt out of synch with my brain. When I'd hopped in the car to make the drive from Ashford, which is an hour from the hospital in Dublin, my body clock was still on New York time. It was about 6 a.m. in Manhattan. I'd barely slept a wink the night before in Room 8 of the Bel Air Hotel, Ashford, the place I've called home in Ireland ever since I broke up with Alan.

I've always wanted to live in a hotel, and the Bel Air, which is mainly an equestrian centre with a riding club, has 12 rooms. It's been run by the same family for the past 60 years, and Fidelma Freeman, the proprietress, is one of my favourite people in the world. But if I had cancer, would a hotel be the place for me, I was thinking as I made my way to the MRI department.

Thinking back, I realise what was strange is how calm and resigned I felt. 'Cancer,' Arnie Hill had said after his professional feel, and I was almost ready to take his word for it. There was no one with me to say otherwise.

Sometimes the great power in being alone is that one can digest bad news without someone else to dramatise the situation. I had no one to tell me not to worry, and, in truth, I wasn't worried, so why bring up that word? I had nobody to jolly me along saying, 'You'll be fine,' as though I wasn't fine. Nothing had actually changed since I'd parked the car and walked through the entrance of the hospital. My physical condition had in no way altered, merely what I knew about it, and the jury was still out. Maybe Arnie Hill was wrong, and maybe the technician operating the mammogram machine was only sending me to MRI for confirmation that I was OK.

The pretty, sophisticated radiologist in the ultrasound unit had served her time at the Sloan Kettering Hospital in New York, as had Arnie Hill. One of my closest friends from college days had had a mastectomy at the Sloan Kettering in August of 2003, and I knew that it was one of the leading cancer units in the States. She was very chatty and recalled Arnie as a young registrar before complimenting me on my diamond earrings. They were the ones I'd received from Mick and worn to his chateau that afternoon I'd first met Keith. I'm hardly the diamond type, but these were nineteenth-century, resembled little daisies and were so subtle that it was interesting that she noticed them while preparing to examine me on the ultrasound machine. It was female stuff and human. She could see me. I was not invisible.

As with Arnie Hill, she struck me as a professional who knew how to appear unrushed, yet judging from the number of people still waiting in the outer office, the poor woman had more appointments than hours in the day. Nonetheless, her open smile and easy banter would have suited a car dealer. In her handsome, well-tailored, black-and-white checked suit, she was trim and stylish, and could have passed for one of those ladies who lunch rather than an overworked hospital radiologist.

Did it matter that her hair was black or that she wore high heels? Her appearance had nothing to do with her ability, but it was all I had to go by, so I studied her out of the corner of my eye as I was removing my shirt and bra to slip on a cotton hospital gown. She was the most senior person in the room, and the friendly nurse in uniform who was assisting had as quick a smile and just as many asides. Since I'm full of chitchat myself, an outside observer might have imagined that we were acquainted.

Having spent the previous month in New York City, where the population appears to come from the crossroads of the world, I was very conscious of being back in Ireland, where I felt I was the only immigrant in the entire country until around 1998, when I started to see the odd Asian and African in Dublin. In the ultrasound unit, I needed to keep in mind that the radiologist was probably friends with at least one person I knew or possibly even related to one. It wasn't a comfort knowing that everybody somehow knows everybody else, and it was equally disconcerting knowing that I was far from anonymous.

My brown skin and long bushy hair made me visible from half a mile in Ireland, and as a writer, I'd received a host of publicity during my nine and a half years in the country, from top TV talk-show appearances to high-profile newspaper and magazine pieces. My last book effort, which was a compilation of writing done by my inmate students at Mountjoy Prison, had caused a lot of controversy because they were almost without exception heroin addicts, and it had been a number-one bestseller in the summer of 1999.

All of this was running through my mind as I sat in that dim room dominated by a machine which was about to do I wasn't sure what, and, rather than ask, my eyes were as wide and expectant as those of any young child that is about to be examined by a big machine.

The screen of the ultrasound machine reminded me of an old-fashioned TV. It was small, about 12 inches by 14 inches, and the image it produced, if you could call it an image, was in black and white. The radiologist was making a few sounds as she ran a cold metal instrument over my right breast and studied the hazy black-and-white image.

'Hmm, yes, there . . .'

'What do you see?' I asked. I don't think my heart skipped a beat, but you couldn't have called me relaxed. 'You see something?'

'Yes. See?' Her slim finger pointed to an area on the screen that looked whiter and denser than the surrounding area. 'There it is.'

There it fucking is.

There it is.

'And here,' she said, moving the instrument towards my underarm. The lymphs. Oh shit. There was no urgency in her voice. No element of emergency. It helped me stay cool, but when I stood up, I saw blood. My blood. From the needle inserted to take a biopsy.

I felt a bit winded. I had some cancer. But whose fault was it? Nobody in that ultrasound room, so I was as light hearted as I might have been had nothing out of the ordinary been seen on the screen.

As I was slipping my black shirt back on, I couldn't even blame Jimi Hendrix.

*Go placidly amidst the noise
and haste and remember what
peace there may be in silence.*

DESIDERATA

3

Tim and Mary

On 16 November 2004, when I dropped into St Vincent's Private Hospital for my lunch-time appointment with Arnie Hill, the breast specialist, I was no novice in dealing with cancer. So I was wearing my diamond earrings to give the impression that I could afford the best. My experience dated back to 1999. That's when my young lover, Alan Gilsenan, for whom I'd moved to Ireland and with whom I'd lived for four years, was diagnosed with colorectal cancer. His being 17 years my junior had nothing to do with why I took over in that situation. It was more to do with how quickly he became too ill to make bold decisions for himself.

The evening in May of '99 that he was admitted to hospital, I was so unimpressed and angry with the circumstances surrounding his cancer diagnosis that, after leaving him, I luckily had the chance to air my angst with my friend, Anne Counihan. Me in a strange house in an unfamiliar city, and Alan in a ward in a public hospital, because he'd forgotten to pay his health insurance . . . My head was swimming. Less than a week earlier, we'd moved out of our place in the Wicklow Mountains to camp temporarily for the summer in Dublin. It was a hellish time for a crisis. There we were, parked at a friend's place, and gorgeous though the house was, smack in the centre of the city, not a stitch in it was ours. That night after leaving him in hospital I was a ship without anchor in a big strange house, in a country that wasn't my own, and with a life-and-death situation that I knew it was up to me to command.

Anne happened to live a few blocks away, and when I'd phoned a few days before to invite her around for a drink, Alan hadn't been diagnosed, let alone admitted to hospital. She's a lawyer by profession and her job with the National Treasury Management probably makes her one of the most powerful women in Ireland. But she hasn't the airs to go with her status and even has that party atmosphere about her that makes her seem like a good-time girl.

We were newish friends, so I had no idea that her father was Professor Tim Counihan, a renowned Dublin heart surgeon. It was just one of those lucky breaks that I'll believe till the day I die saved my boyfriend's life.

Now, although none of this was specifically going through my head that November afternoon in 2004 when I went to see the breast specialist, the truth is some experiences, like coping with Alan's unexpected cancer diagnosis, never leave you. They immerse themselves into your being so that the memory plays in and out countless times with the ease and naturalness of your heartbeat.

Miss Anne Counihan's a goer and doer, and that night when she dropped by for a glass of wine, I was anxious and even angry as I retold the two years of events that led up to Alan being in hospital under the care of a surgeon he'd seen twice but who'd misdiagnosed his chronic symptoms.

'And now,' I told Anne, 'the same guy's gonna take a knife to him.'

Tim and Mary

Anne said, 'That doesn't sound right.'

'Can you believe it? Alan. The 6 ft 2 in. 400 m runner. Thirty-seven. Gym fanatic. Cancer . . .'

As I ranted, Anne was checking her watch. 'Guess it's not too late to ring the parents. You need to talk to Dad.'

Something about the way she pronounced 'Dad' had a ring that was similar to the way believers say God.

Anne explained that her mother, Mary, had also been a young doctor when she married Tim Counihan, who wasn't then a surgeon. But Mary dropped medicine to raise their children, Anne being the eldest, with three brothers.

I wish I could remember the exact date, because that's when Tim and Mary Counihan came into my life. What happened that night not only saved Alan but also saved me.

What complicated Alan being diagnosed with cancer and hospitalised was our residential situation. We were on the move and between homes. Having left the big house we'd been renting in the mountains outside Dublin, a friend of mine in London was lending us her three-storey Dublin house. Having put everything, including most of my clothes, in storage, Alan and I were living out of suitcases. While Anne was dialling her parents, I was as much a stranger in that exquisite yellow sitting room as she was. I like feeling in control, being in the know, but there I was a foreigner, unschooled in the ways of Irish hospitals, while my boyfriend was a few miles away spending his first night in a public ward with five elderly patients. That his mother had been diagnosed with cancer the previous year at that same hospital made me all the more anxious. Though she died soon after in a hospice, I knew that, psychologically, it was not a good place for Alan to be.

Anne apologised to her mother for ringing so late. Unfortunately, Tim, Anne's father was in Edinburgh, testing future doctors, and couldn't be reached until the morning. That gave me a long, gruelling night to roll the notion of cancer around in my mind. It carries with it the terrors of pain and long-term suffering and the unknown factors of chemotherapy, not to mention death.

Cancer. Fucking cancer . . . And it was not only his problem, it was now mine, because he was on his back and he was mine.

I sensed it was no time to panic but to view the situation as one would an enemy. Therein was the value of having started life in a tough, inner-city American ghetto. My mental attitude is a street fighter's approach. I face an obstacle and it's 'OK, motherfucka, throw down!' And the fight's on.

I didn't know what to expect when I called Professor Counihan in Edinburgh the following morning. Anne was a relatively new friend – what could I ask of him? What could he tell me? As I stood in the basement kitchen of that tall, old Dublin house, I gritted my teeth, took a deep breath and tried to keep my hand from shaking. I wasn't aware that I was about to begin the most crucial aspect of dealing with cancer: I was about to talk to a surgeon, renowned and respected, more revered than a priest, and I was going to have to engage him in a medical discussion in laymen's terms, so that I could understand enough to make decisions and judgements about another person's life. It was daunting, and the fact that my deceased father had been a doctor, a psychiatrist, didn't erase my sense of physicians being a mysterious clan, a powerful cartel.

Professor Counihan not only took the time to recommend what I might do, he also suggested that I ring a colleague of his at the Mater Private Hospital in Dublin who might take on Alan's case. That was encouraging, because I was eager to get Alan to a private hospital, because he's so private. I'd explained that being in a public ward was probably bad for his psyche and he needed a healthy one to recover.

From that morning on, I remained so grateful to Professor Counihan for giving us a new direction that I made a point of keeping him informed about Alan's progress. Nothing intrusive. Just a note from time to time from the moment I had Alan moved from St Vincent's Teaching Hospital to the Mater Private, where Tim was a senior consultant. I continued to do so even after my split with Alan in January 2000, aware that their advice at a crucial time had been instrumental in saving his life. I had no idea that when I dropped Tim and his wife, Mary, a line about Alan's marriage in 2003 and the birth of his daughter in April 2004, in due course I'd be calling on them to save mine. Keeping them informed was a way of reminding them that they'd not only helped to save his life but were indirectly instrumental in him forming happy new bonds and creating a new life.

On 16 November 2004, when I had the lunch-time appointment with Arnie Hill, only six months had lapsed since I'd sent a card to Tim and Mary about the birth of Alan's daughter.

The canteen at St Vincent's Private Hospital is both modest and a modest size. The area cordoned off for hospital staff is no bigger than a small café. The reason I chose to sit in the corner furthest from it had nothing to do with the nurses sitting there in their uniforms. I didn't want to be near anybody, and the round table in the corner near the window looked as isolated and removed from the canteen as I was feeling.

Breast cancer.

Me, with breast cancer.

'Wellsy-dellsy,' I was thinking. It's an expression my mother used when I was a kid to limit the blow of bad news. Somehow wellsy-dellsy kept everything in order, under control, tinged it with a hint of folksy comedy, leaving no room for high drama to grab the situation and run away with it.

Being late afternoon and tea time, I had every excuse for leaving the ultrasound room and heading down to the hospital's canteen for tea and cake. That there was lemon cake, my favourite, seemed a good omen, and as I headed for the table in the far corner by the window, I was replaying a memory of that afternoon in the spring of '99 when Alan was diagnosed with cancer. I was recalling how I'd been waiting in the public reception and working on my laptop as he emerged from his meeting with the surgeon with news that the tumour he had was malignant. Alan's tall, well built and handsome, a noticeable figure in any crowd, and though he appeared healthy, there he was carrying a lethal disease and had been for some time. I looked up and didn't know what to say to him, in that way one is lost for words and even true feelings the moment you hear that someone you know has died. Alan with cancer?

Having driven to a nearby hotel to mull over the shocking news in the dimly lit lounge bar, I cried before my Guinness was served. And I have to own up that I wasn't only crying for him, I was crying for myself. Because I knew that as able a film-maker as he was, he wasn't the sort that knew how to deal with doctors, let alone hospitals. I wept for both of us and for the fact that, since he'd forgotten to pay his health insurance, we were in for a tough ride.

I'm sloppy about paying bills. But Alan's experience made me never forget to pay my health insurance. Five and a half years later, I was still vigilant. In fact, a letter from my insurers had arrived for me that morning as I dressed for my appointment with Arnie Hill.

Tim and Mary

Sitting alone in the canteen of St Vincent's Private Hospital with my tea and lemon cake, I had no tears, no sadness, no remorse. I knew that I'd made a choice and, having chosen my book above my life, had to now live with the consequences. Had I killed myself? Had I meant to? A host of silly questions popped in and out of my head, and a moment came to mind from 1999 when I told an architect friend of ours, Peter White, that Alan had cancer.

'He'll be fine,' I said. 'I think I'm up for it.'

'No better woman,' Peter smiled. I knew that he meant it and his belief in me empowered me then. Now, as I sat in the canteen of St Vincent's, sipping my tea and taking a bite of lemon cake, the memory of his words empowered me again.

Wellsy-dellsy.

No better woman. But I knew that feeling empowered wouldn't necessarily keep me alive, because cancer can be a killer. Still, Alan wasn't dead. In fact, he'd had his five-year check and been given a clean bill of health, and I could see that in important ways cancer had resurrected his life, led him to become a husband and father, reminded his family and colleagues how valuable he was to their lives . . . And having served as his advocate, minded his back, surely I could mind my own.

I've always thought that the real bonus about having grown up Negro in America is that there was that unrelenting training throughout childhood and into the teenage years that forced an early maturity. You had to face early on the fact that life could be hard, cruel and sometimes so shockingly ugly. You learned that the trick of endurance was to find your groove, find the irony when the shit got grotesque, and never be surprised when life reared up and gave you an undeserved kick in the ass. But there in a Dublin hospital, without another brown face in the canteen, I was a long way from American apartheid and felt so far from home as I swallowed another sip of tea. I scratched my head as I tend to do when I'm tired. Was it jet lag or life that had tired me? I couldn't say, and were you to ask what most defined my mood at that moment I'd say it was a quietness.

My breathing was even, and I was still inside. Neither empty nor blank. Neither sad nor scared. No anger. No rage. I understood that having made my bed I had to lie in it, while doing my utmost to stay alive.

Time. I'd given cancer time to fester. For Jimi's sake, I'd let a tumour grow and grow. There was no avoiding this fact as I sat at the table and poured a second cup of tea from the pot, this time emptying three packets of sugar into the cup as though the sweetness was a panacea for my condition. And maybe it was, since I had not one but two major things to deal with. What seemed more important than the state of my breast, about which I could do fuck all that afternoon, was my state of mind. I needed an approach to hold me strong for whatever was going to happen.

Though some might argue that immediately eliminating sugar from my diet was crucial, I figured I possibly needed that hot sugary drink to stave off shock, as one would after a car crash. Because was I in shock? Is that why I'd remained so calm in the face of the cancer verdict? I looked for signs. I didn't seem shaky, and my hand was perfectly steady as I brought the teacup to my lips. I had no butterflies in my stomach and no trouble downing the sweet but tart lemon cake. In fact, if truth be known, each bite contented me. The lemony flavour, the soothing warmth of the milky tea, the sight of people, hospital and canteen staff moving about quietly amongst the odd concerned-looking visitor. Hospital, a place of death as well as healing, and people still needed their coffee, still needed the momentary buzz of a chocolate bar or maybe some lemon cake.

Eventually, with no more than a few crumbs left on the saucer, I needed to make a move and instinctively knew that it was one of those times when it was unhealthy to be alone. So, after clearing my place, I stopped at the cashier's to get change for the public pay phone to ring Tim and Mary.

Being a writer, I need aloneness, relish it, seek it and value it. I see silence as being an essential tool for my work. In the past 20 years, I've learned to embrace isolation like others embrace lovers. I let it wrap itself around me and will bury myself in it night and day, day after day, without even a phone call to break the solitude. But there's a part of me, that part that was a singer and actress, which is equally a people person and I can cling like moss to friends, wallow in conversation and thrive on feeling myself laugh at somebody's mad banter. And at that moment, aware that cancer was clutching my right bosom, I didn't think it wise to drive back alone to the Wicklow Mountains, where I was staying. Maybe I wanted to retrace some of the steps that I'd made as Alan's cancer partner. I can't say why I did what I did, but, with hindsight, I'd say that it was the right thing. Maybe I wanted to be in the presence of two old and wise medics, trained to deal with illness and fearless of death, if not their own, that of others, because it struck me that, as well as I felt apart from my breast, maybe I was dying.

Shrewsbury Road is the best address in Dublin. It's in Ballsbridge, near the British Embassy and the Four Seasons Hotel, and it's only a couple of blocks long. The houses are large and set back from the street and generally have drives in front with a bit of landscaped garden. There's rarely a sign of anybody walking, even though the Chester Beatty Museum, which houses a collection of Asian art, is almost directly opposite the tree-lined drive leading to Tim and Mary's.

Tim's such a young name, and Professor Tim Counihan has such a young smile, that it seems incongruous that he's 82. When he answered the front door, we were both grinning from ear to ear, my smile pumping up his, and his, in turn, pumping up mine. There he stood, thinning hair and glasses, a heart surgeon, now retired, who had saved lives every one of his working days as a matter of course. It enraged me to think that society is so stupid that now, like some great thoroughbred racer, life was preparing Tim for the knacker's yard. All that knowledge and experience, 50 years of a bedside manner, left to read the papers and potter about the large garden.

'How lovely to see you, Tim,' I said, handing him a bouquet of flowers.

'Oh, Marsha, you shouldn't have,' he said and seemed to mean it.

'Of course I should've.'

My life is full of crazy coincidences, bizarre connections, queer serendipity, and one of the odd things that came up years ago when talking to Tim is that he was a young intern at Boston General Hospital around the same time as my father. Though it was too long ago for Tim to recall the other young house doctors, the fact that my father had been there gave Tim and I some common ground that probably raised my standing in his eyes through the unlikely association.

Following him into the spacious living room, I was still clutching the small, gift-wrapped cookies that I'd also brought him and Mary. I forgot to hand them over until he left me to get her and ask their housekeeper, Roisin, to bring tea. As I settled into the low chintz chair that faces their light, flower-lined conservatory, I knew I'd come to the right place. No sign of a TV or newspaper. No music playing. And, best of all, no sign, thank God, of Christmas, which, though more than five weeks away, was rearing its head in the streets and stores.

Though the room wasn't chilly, I didn't remove my black

leather jacket and sat perched on the edge of the seat, preoccupied with the knowledge that I had cancer and needed to both let the reality of that sink in while at the same time holding it at bay until I had a game plan. In the past hour, my life had totally altered, and I alone held the power to determine how things would play out. Was Arnie Hill the right surgeon for me? Was St Vincent's Private Hospital the right hospital for me? What to do next was on my mind when Tim re-entered the living room, soon followed by Mary, and before long, Roisin came in carrying a silver tray with pretty cups and saucers.

On previous visits to the Counihans, and I'd only been twice, I'd sat on the sofa facing the fireplace. But as in the hospital canteen, this time I'd chosen a chair that set me apart, gave me space and distance, let me be there yet somehow stand apart. Though nothing about me had changed since the morning, apart from the information I had about myself, I felt cautious about mingling.

Cancer . . . breast . . . Cancer . . . life . . . Cancer . . . death . . . Cancer . . . me . . .

Cancer . . . I wanted to take it seriously, but 'wellsy-dellsy' kept putting it in its place as Mary eased her way into the room, walking slowly and barely using her cane, while her brunette hair flipped my thoughts miles away to my brunette buddy, Patricia, in New York who'd had a mastectomy the previous summer and was thriving.

'Mary,' I smiled, rising from my seat, 'how do you do it? Always so pretty.'

I marvel at elderly women who keep up appearances, and Mary always looked like she'd spent the morning at the hairdresser's and gone straight from there to have somebody do her make-up. Her exotic earrings looked just right with her silk kimono, both of which she said were gifts from Anne.

Mary has a smoker's voice, with that sexy hint of gravel in it that compliments her sophistication. Despite my ten years in Ireland, I'm still unable to locate an accent, and although Mary originates from Cork, she sounds like a wealthy Dublin dowager to me.

'How are you, Marsha?' she asked.

Weird how that time-worn greeting took me by surprise and raised my emotion to such a sudden pitch that I feared I might cry. It demanded a simple truth that I wasn't prepared to share. Whether it was self-pity that rose in my throat and gagged me or what sounded like Mary's genuine interest in my well-being, it rendered me so speechless I could barely get out the word 'fine'. It sounded so rude as it flew at her across the room with no added thank you and no complementary 'and how are you?'

I'd arrived with no intention of saying that I'd just found out I had cancer, because I remembered from my experience with Alan years earlier that mentioning the word could put him on the receiving end of God knows what, ranging from outpourings of sympathy that lay in his lap like a dead pet, through fearful stares which made it seem that he had a contagious disease, to the worst responses of all, which were the long, long stories about somebody else's cancer that had resulted in a horrible death. No, I sensed that I was not yet comfortable enough with the notion that I had breast cancer to share it with anyone. Not even the very learned and civilised medical couple, Tim and Mary.

Maybe what I'd really come for was tea and company as opposed to tea and sympathy. Roisin set it out so beautifully on the silver tray with the delicate china cups, and the expensive, handmade cookies I'd bought added some extra pizzazz to the overall presentation. Had there been a roaring fire in the grate, I might have removed my coat and begged to stay the night. As it was, the hour I spent was just perfect. I had no mother and father, and they would do. Not as replacements as such but as my older generation.

'How's the book going?' Tim asked.

'Jimi and I are still a couple,' I laughed. 'In January, it will be five years in the writing, and although there was a time when people saw some merit in taking time to write a book, now friends shake their heads when they hear I'm still not finished. They think I'm retarded. And maybe they're right. I know two people who started their Ph.D.s and have completed them in the time that I've been working on this book. People have been born and died. Kids have started high school and since graduated. And I'm still at it, and all the more convinced that I witnessed a time in history that's re-evaluated by observing it through Jimi's life. And, Tim!' I gave him a school-marmish look, 'What about *your* book?'

This serious surgeon always manages a giggle when I ask, since the idea that he should write his life story remains only mine and that of his daughter, Anne.

I turned to Mary, who was lighting her second cigarette. Each only lasts a few minutes, because she's too ladylike to smoke them down to the filter. 'Mary, why don't you help? How about I bring a little tape recorder?'

When Tim leaves the planet, a piece of oral history about the medical profession in Ireland will go with him. And what profession could tell more about the people?

Tim and Mary. Seeing them reminded me of the gruelling cancer journey that I'd made with Alan. Seeing them recalled our success. Tim. This brilliant mind, this lifetime of experience: a heart man, here in this quiet room with his attention focused upon my visit. And me. Alone. Not saying much of anything but comforted by him and Mary being alive. These two good people were unknowingly waving me off on a dangerous journey called cancer.

Do what you can, where you are,
with what you have.

THEODORE ROOSEVELT

4

The Bel Air Hotel

'Hey, Mama,' said Karis. 'Where are you?'

'Ireland. The dear ol' Bel Air.' I was sounding so upbeat, she couldn't have guessed that I harboured bad news. 'How's by you? Jonathan home yet?' My 2 a.m. in Ireland was 6 p.m. for her in LA.

Only five days earlier, I'd been at JFK airport in New York and had rung her to say that I was about to board the plane and fly back to Europe. She knew Ireland well, because she'd visited me more than a few times, and in 2001, while she was pregnant with Mazie, and her husband, Jonathan, was shooting a movie just outside of Dublin, they'd taken an apartment in the city for four months.

Karis wasn't big on answering the phone, so I was sort of taken aback to suddenly hear her voice. I knew that she was probably organising Mazie's supper and that Jonathan, who was working on a Hollywood movie, wouldn't have arrived home yet from Universal Studios across town. I'd finally mustered up the courage to tap out her number after pacing up and down Room 8 of the Bel Air Hotel endless times, but no sooner than I heard her say 'Mama', somehow my confidence took a nose dive.

I was using my mobile phone while sitting on the edge of the bed that's nearest the wall of the tall Victorian windows. Room 8 is my favourite not only because it's spacious but because the windows overlook both the hotel's handsome forecourt and the beautiful green meadow beyond, which is usually littered with either sheep or cows, depending on the weather. The spectacular view stretches from the small town of Ashford in County Wicklow straight out to the Irish Sea. It's glorious even when the sky is the bleakest grey or it's raining. Or both. But when I rang Karis, it was too pitch black out to see more than the headlights of a car in the far distance speeding along the newly opened motorway.

Often when I have something difficult to relay in a phone call, I jot some notes to myself and keep them in front of me, so I don't forget what I've rung to say, or, better still, I have a little speech prepared. Though I never do that with Karis, on hearing her voice I suddenly regretted that I hadn't. I didn't want to sound ridiculously casual, as my mother had in '99 when she'd rung me in Ireland to say that she had lung cancer. I eventually realised with hindsight that she too must have been stumped by how to break the news, and that she too was alone when she'd rung to tell me.

'Well, Pepperpot,' she'd said cheerfully, addressing me by an old nickname, 'I've got the big C.'

'The big C?' I'd snorted, a bit grumpy that she was speaking in code.

'Cancer,' she'd said, like she might've said she'd picked up a six-pack of Coke.

She'd gone to the extreme of making it sound like it was

nothing because she obviously didn't know how to break the news to me about her terminal lung cancer.

Now, five years later, there I was in the same predicament. How do you tell your kid that you have a killer disease? I didn't know how to begin and started in the worst way possible.

'Listen, I don't want you to worry,' I told Karis, 'but I've got a bit of shitty news.'

No sooner than the words left my mouth, I thought, 'Dickhead! Why'd you start this sounding like the voice of doom? She's doesn't need the aggravation. Stay up . . . keep it light, because there's damn all she can do but worry.'

I'd been tempted not to tell Karis. She was eight months pregnant, and hearing on the phone that I had cancer was the last thing that she needed. Yet not to tell her would have been equally dreadful and could have broken the trust that I've spent her lifetime building by always being honest with her. There's also a pecking order for certain kinds of news, and I was sure that it wouldn't have been right not to tell her before telling my brother, Dennis, who also lives in LA and visits her regularly.

Where I'm concerned, I loathe giving Karis anything but news that will make me seem a winner able to cope under all circumstances. This is partly to do with her being my only child and next of kin. I don't want her to think that as I age I might become a burden. Plus there's the issue of my male counterpart, her father, Mick, who's now in his early 60s and seems to be going from strength to strength as he ages. His financial future is secure, and she doesn't ever have to think for a second that she could wind up having to take care of him. Though Karis, being Karis, would never openly admit that my being broke bothers her, it must.

Over the past ten years, she's been good about lending me

money, so since my first consultation with Arnie Hill it had continuously preyed on my mind that were I to croak from breast cancer, how would she get back the thousands that she'd lent me? That worry was also behind me continuing to write my Hendrix book, believing as I did that it would be the work which allowed me to repay her.

If I haven't already said it, know that until she was grown, I'd lived my life for my daughter. Every minute of every day, I tried to be the best mother I could be *because* I was a single working mother in show business, where the tradition of putting one's kids after one's career was not only expected but respected. So nobody gave me any points for turning down jobs and even publicity that I felt wouldn't benefit her.

When I say that she raised me and was my greatest blessing, I'm merely stating facts. But nowadays my shaky finances have everything to do with putting her first from the time that I was 23 until I was 44, although others might argue that with her having reached adulthood, I then opted for a writing career that was even more precarious than singing and acting.

It's cost me dearly. I've had to tighten my belt more and more as the years have gone by and have even been unable to keep up with mortgage payments and lost valuable property to continue being a writer. But the truth is that as soon as I turned 40, I knew that in the long run, pursuing a writing career was saner, safer and way more fulfilling than acting. There was almost a certainty that acting jobs would be fewer and further between as I got older.

Maybe it was seeing how often I struggled to pay bills that made Karis choose the traditional homemaker role for herself. She and Jonathan have a wonderful life in LA, where he gets back-to-back work as a first assistant director in the movie business and she gave up work as a production assistant so that she could stay home and raise their kids. But it was about to become less wonderful, I imagined, when she had to take on board that I had breast cancer, while her baby was due at the end of December.

I could hear three-year-old Mazie in the background as I mustered up the courage to splurt, 'Listen, I've got breast cancer. But the good news is that I've kept up my health insurance.' I was proud to be able to add that last sentence, because, five years earlier, when I'd announced that Alan had cancer, I'd also had to say that he'd forgotten to pay his health insurance.

On that occasion, I was crying. This time around, Karis was.

It hurt to hear my granddaughter. 'What's wrong, Mom . . . Mom, what's wrong?' she was asking her mother.

'My mama's sick,' Karis was telling her.

Whatever reaction I was expecting from my daughter, somehow it wasn't that. She's normally calm. Hearing her upset nearly unravelled me. But I was determined not to cry.

'Listen, breast cancer's no big deal. People get it all the time. I'll be fine.'

'But I can't come to take care of you, Mama. I can't fly. I'm due in six weeks.'

In the background, Mazie was still asking what was wrong. I could just imagine her little face, those big dark eyes searching her mother's.

There's nobody living that I've loved as much as my daughter. Yet when it came to deferring my breast examination in favour of finishing my Hendrix book, I decided that having lived my life for my girl, now that she had a family of her own and no real dependence upon me, it was time that I thought about myself.

After Karis finished Yale in '92 and decided to settle in San

Francisco, the closeness that we'd shared throughout her childhood and teen years had begun to shift. It sometimes felt that our past had become little more than photos of us together dating back to her birth. And since graduating from college, Karis had grown equally close to Mick and his large brood, including Bianca's daughter, Jade, and Jerry's four kids. Now, separated by 6,000 miles and that mysterious measure called time, Karis was building an American family of her own.

While we were on the phone, her evening was just beginning. Rush hour in LA. Dusk in the warm, leafy hills of Laurel Canyon. But there in the wee hours of the morning in the Bel Air Hotel there was that heavy country silence. Nothing stirred.

The joy of staying at the Bel Air is that it required nothing of me on my return. No plants to water. No beds to air. Just the pile of mail waiting for me and a warm welcome from Fidelma Freeman and her family. I could slip back into Room 8 and find it just as I'd left it. Cupboards and drawers waiting to be filled. Chocolate biscuits on the plate beside the clean cup and saucer, with everything I needed to brew a cup of tea. I am my home. But there was a time when Karis was my home.

My voice seemed incredibly out of place as I explained to her how simple the mastectomy would be and how lucky I was to be in Ireland, where I had friends and a support system that would mean that her absence wasn't leaving me in the lurch.

'I wasn't doing a damn thing with that breast. Ain't no big deal that it's goin'.'

I liked the sound of that so much that I was going to repeat it to my brother, Dennis, when I called him, and to my dear friend, Dana Wynter, when I called her, and again to Mick when I called him to say that Karis was upset by my news and could he ring her.

Mick was quiet when I rang him. The word cancer seems to temper people.

'I'll be fine,' I said, sounding almost jolly.

'Can I do anything?'

'Yeah. I need to talk to Keith about Jimi.'

Bitch. Was I that ambitious for this book? Obviously so.

'I've no say in what Keith does,' said Mick.

'I know. But could you ask him? I've put years into this fucking book. And in case I'm on the way out of here, I want it to be my best. It would be great if I could talk to Keith.'

'Yeah. But I can't promise anything. It's up to Keith.'

OK. It was a cheap shot. Poor Mick. Put on the spot. But you've got to put yourself in my shoes. For all I knew, sitting there in Room 8, I was dying, and there was no certainty about how much time I had left. And in case I'd actually cut my life short for the sake of the book I was writing, now I had to create every chance to make it the truest witness that I could provide. That meant talking to Keith, and I was prepared to crawl to get to him.

Half the beauty of Room 8 at the Bel Air is in the dimensions of the room and its long adjoining bathroom. The ceilings are very high and the view from the window seems to extend the room beyond its walls to include the view outside. At night, I can pull up a chair and watch the moon and stars. But that wasn't the night for star gazing. I wanted to be efficient, to use my time well. I was suddenly so conscious of each minute passing and the various people I wanted to tell. Again, Alan's cancer had been something of a rehearsal for my own, as I recalled how we'd made a list of who needed to hear directly that he was ill.

Don't waste any time in mourning. Organise!

JOE HILL

5

Body and Soul

It was Friday, 19 November, three days after my first meeting with Arnie Hill.

I was sitting in a large reception area of St Vincent's Private Hospital waiting to see him for the second time to get the results of my biopsy. That line from an Emily Dickinson poem kept going through my head: *because I could not stop for death, it kindly stopped for me.* What was annoying was that I couldn't for the life of me remember the rest of it.

To be honest, the notion of dying, of no longer being here, didn't bother me, probably for a lot of reasons. One is that I spend a lot of time in graveyards, because the area of northern France where I have the writing studio is in the heart of the killing fields of the First World War and every other village seems to have a designated burial ground for British soldiers killed in that conflict. I often stop and say a prayer for all the young soldiers. Plus I was brought up by women, my mother, her sister and their mother, who all strongly believed in spirits and the afterlife, so it's not surprising that I do. Plus there's the fact that my grandmother's daily rant was, 'I ain't scared of a sonuvabitch living and I ain't scared to die!' I must have heard her repeat that as often when I was growing up as I heard the weather forecast on the radio. I lit candles for the dead on a daily basis. Prayed for them and asked for their guidance. So to think that I might join their number didn't trouble me.

With that said, however, nor was I sitting there in the reception of St Vincent's Private in any hurry to die. I had every intention of trying to keep myself alive but knew very well that, despite feeling healthy, my body was possibly riddled with cancer and I already had one foot in the grave. I'd braced myself to hear that I had breast cancer, but possibly the news was worse and it had metastasised. Though I could spell that word, I got tongue tied trying to pronounce it, which might have had something to do with how I imagined it might have applied to me.

Metastasise . . . the dreaded cancer spread . . . The tenderness in the lower left side of my right breast was no more than that: a tenderness, and what's interesting was that, despite how well I felt in general, I harboured a killing disease. There I was. Philadelphia born, California bred, 30 years of my life spent in Britain, London mainly, where I'd become an adult, made my name, raised Karis, practised my professions. And now I was in the shit in Dublin.

I'd been sitting there in that spacious, handsomely decorated reception area for over 45 minutes and was in no hurry for my turn with Arnie Hill. I had no other appointments that Friday afternoon. Occasionally he'd appear near the water dispenser and beckon someone else waiting for him, and I knew that with my bush of hair and dark skin there was no way that he could have failed to notice me.

I guess it was natural that along with replaying that Emily

Dickinson line, I sat recalling things that had happened during the previous six months which flagged that I was in trouble. Like the way the colour around my nipple had changed from deep brown to a paler shade. I thought I was imagining it and looking in the mirror after my bath I'd try to remember what the colour had been before. Then I thought about how I'd gone to that big, fancy homoeopathic store a block from Grand Central Station in New York to pick up a remedy called carcinogen, which my homoeopath said would reduce that swelling. How excited I'd been that they had it in stock and let me see the book about remedies which explained that it was for swollen mammary glands. I took it faithfully for the month I was in New York, surfing the net from time to time for info about mammograms and breast cancer. 'Marsha, you're not the cancer type,' my homoeopath had said. But there I was at St Vincent's Private proving her wrong.

It hardly looked like a hospital reception and definitely didn't smell like one. A very large tapestry, which I thought was meant to be the tree of life, nearly covered the whole of one wall. There was none of that heavy scent of disinfectant or chloroform, no signs of gurneys or wheelchairs, of nurses or doctors. No atmosphere of urgency. I could have been sitting in the reception of a slick publishing house or an insurance company. Obviously some top architect and first-class interior decorator had gone to lengths to eliminate the feeling that this was a place of sickness and recovery, surgery and death.

On an overhead TV in the corner, a pretty English presenter was spewing out what we've grown to accept as news. Tempted though I was to watch, I averted my eyes, resisting the sound and colour, the images and voices. Nor did I skim through the dog-eared celebrity magazines. Tom Cruise was smiling on the cover of one, an ex-Spice girl filled the cover of another and on a third, resting on the edge of a coffee table, was a collection of faces that I couldn't name. Maybe they were soap stars or from one of the 'reality' TV shows. I pride myself in refusing to let the media draw my focus away from real life.

There were several other women waiting to be seen, but I was the only black one and the only one alone. Two had women with them. Three had men. Nearest me sat a tall man in a pinstriped suit who was with a woman almost as lean and lanky as he. While she sat on the edge of her seat, their expressions were grim and they made no effort to speak to each other. Her anxiety seemed to creep about the room, and I shifted in my seat, hoping that it wouldn't stop at me. Her headscarf barely hid the fact that she was bald and her pallor had to be due to illness. She was too colourless to be well.

A cancer patient no doubt.

Would I soon look like that? Was it possible to be poisoned by the chemicals of chemotherapy flushing through your system and still look healthy?

Since my first appointment with Arnie Hill three days earlier, I'd been gearing myself up for this second appointment and arrived at the St Vincent's Private Hospital wearing the diamond earrings again, in case I was going to meet somebody else who would be involved in my cancer treatment.

For three days, ever since Tuesday, when Arnie Hill had felt the lump in my breast and said, 'I think this is cancer,' the notion of dying had occupied my thoughts. I'd been thinking that, if I had to die, Ireland was a good place, since the Irish, Irish Catholics in particular, do death so well. They've made it so much their thing that it verges on becoming a social art form.

I considered myself lucky having had a chance to see first

hand how Alan's mother, Isabel, had conducted herself from the day her cancer was diagnosed, how she died from it and was buried. It wasn't long after Easter, when Isabel had been out to stay with us at the wonderful house we had in Roundwood, that she was told she had liver cancer. She was an in-patient in a ward at St Vincent's Teaching Hospital and when she got the news, she told Alan, very matter of factly, 'You'll have to ring Our Lady's.' That was the hospice where a distant cousin of hers, Sister Ignatius, was a member of the staff. And sure enough, that's where Isabel was moved to, telling Alan on the drive there that she wanted me to wear my hair back at her funeral and dictating what she wanted served at the luncheon following her burial. It seemed such a swell way to go that it was no doubt contributing to my relative calm about my own situation. If Arnie said I was a terminal case, I was going to ring Sister Ignatius.

But he didn't.

'This is treatable,' Arnie smiled, when I was finally in for my consultation. The nurse in the room with him was the hospital's breast-care nurse. Her name was Claire, and I would soon discover that breast-care nurses are a crucial part of the medical team that deal with breast cancer. Claire seemed as relaxed and friendly as Arnie, so I didn't mind when he said that I'd be seeing a lot of her. Her pleasant face was set off by neatly cropped brown hair. She looked efficient in her uniform, and though Arnie did most of the talking, she added a few words now and then.

I was going to have to wait to find out to what extent the cancer had metastasised into my lymph glands. Arnie didn't mind me calling him Arnie, and when he asked whether I wanted to have breast reconstruction when the tumour was removed, I may have surprised him with my answer.

'Absolutely not.' I was positive. Why subject my body to more surgery than was necessary? 'I have no problem with having one breast. The Amazons did, right? So I'll be an Amazon. What the hell. My problem is that my daughter has a baby due at the end of December, and I don't want her worried until then that I might be dying from cancer. So how soon can I get this done?'

An unspoken nightmare in this scenario which I hadn't made allowances for is that the Irish are big into Christmas, which was five weeks away at that point but seemed to be setting upon us faster than the speed of light. While I was speaking with Arnie and the breast-care nurse, Christmas hadn't crossed my mind, but no doubt it had crossed theirs, as Arnie looked at his diary and said, 'The 30th. November 30th. You'd come in the evening before. The 29th.'

Shit.

Now, in case, you're forgetting, remember that I'd only been back from New York for five days. My being there for a month meant that my body clock was still on New York time, and I hadn't yet settled into any normal routine. Until my appointment with Arnie Hill few days earlier, the most important thing in my life was a book that I'd been working on for nearly five years. Due to that commitment, without a publisher underwriting my expenses, I was broke. Alone and broke. And due to jet lag, at that moment, I was tired, alone and broke. But I had something going for me, which nobody will understand unless they've shared the experience: I grew up a Negro child in the United States, and nobody but nobody ever said life was going to be anything else but a struggle against heavy odds. So, instead of falling apart that Friday in the office with Arnie and Claire, the American Negro in me kicked in. I call it those good old slave genes, which may not be politically correct, but it's no less the case.

So I'm sitting in that office, which is so sterile that it strikes me as one that the hospital doctors must use on a rota, and I'm faced with Arnie and Claire, and the new fact that in ten days I will go under his knife. 'Fabulous,' I said, and meant it. 'Ten days. Let's do it. And by the way, I hear you've got triplets. True?'

The radiologist who gave me my ultrasound examination three days earlier had mentioned that Arnie Hill was the father of four boys under six and that three are four-year-old triplets. It was hard not to admire him for merely facing the day.

Claire and I watched while he reached in his pocket and pulled out his mobile phone. 'Look,' he said, his pretty surgeon's hands fumbling with a couple of buttons until the small screen on the phone reflected the moving images of four little boys romping outdoors.

Arnie's eyes gleamed with such pride that it was touching. He was young enough to be my son and yet had so much responsibility, for these small sons and for so many other lives, including now mine.

I felt sure that I'd done the right thing in returning to Ireland to have my condition diagnosed rather than having tests in New York, where apartheid rules. To be an African-American of late middle age, unknown in that teeming city, would definitely not have got me the first-class treatment that I'd been receiving from the moment I met Mr Hill. Yet I was also sure that my American upbringing made me the warrior I needed to be to do cancer on my own, to watch my own back and be the advocate for myself that I'd been for Alan. How wrong I was.

Life does not consist mainly – or even largely – of facts and happenings. It consists mainly of the storms that are forever blowing through one's mind.

MARK TWAIN

6

Hair Today, Gone Tomorrow

The instant that Arnie Hill confirmed that I had breast cancer and said that the chemotherapy needed after surgery would render me bald, I was less concerned about losing a breast or my life than I was about what Baby Girl would make of me without my bushy mane.

Her full name is Mazie Rane Watson, but I nicknamed her 'Baby Girl' from the moment that she was born. It was 25 July 2001, and, though she arrived two weeks early, by some incredible fluke Mick and I were both in the delivery room at Cedars Sinai Hospital in LA when Karis gave birth to her. I'd been working on my Hendrix book for 19 months and had just driven from Vegas the night before, where I'd been interviewing Jimi's Harlem girlfriend. Mick had come in from Miami to record in Hollywood. When we stood side by side watching an African-American obstetrician named Dr Hendrix pull Mazie into the world, it struck me as eerie that he not only had Jimi's name and spelled it the same but looked a bit like Jimi. What was also strange is that when Karis told me that she was pregnant and due in August, I predicted that the baby would arrive on Mick's birthday, which it was according to Greenwich Mean Time.

I knew that this baby would become a special person in my life from the moment I saw Dr Hendrix easing her head from my daughter's womb. People now say she looks like Karis, but from day one she was the double of her father. From her cowlick to her toenails, she's the spitting image of Jonathan. I called her 'Baby Girl' to bring a touch of the ghetto to her highly middle-class reality. Baby Girl Watson has a sound of street to it that will keep me centred about her, even if it doesn't keep her feeling centred herself. And I asked that she call me Grammy, which sounded cute to me for a while, but then, down the line, I wanted something hipper, like Bootsy, but she's refused to move from Grammy. Our living 6,000 miles apart doesn't afford me much chance to play a grandmother's role, and though I've managed to visit a few times, she hasn't seen much of me since she was born.

By 1 August 2004, when she and Karis flew into Charles de Gaulle airport near Paris, to hang out with me for a week at my writing studio, Baby Girl had just turned three and hadn't seen me since she was twenty months. Kids that age are wary of strangers, which I was as far as she was concerned, so I knew better than to try to hug her. When she and Karis emerged from passport control at 9 a.m., after a ten-hour flight, Karis had her in a pushchair, and I acted like I barely noticed Baby Girl until Karis said, 'There's a toilet. Will you watch her for a sec, Mum?'

Baby Girl was in pink plimsolls and olive-green trousers that looked like they were designed for combat. She was unbearably pretty with her big saucer eyes and dark wavy hair, a sort of mini Gina Lollobrigida. But I knew better than to touch her or even look too hard at her. She didn't look at me and sat silent and motionless in her lightweight American pushchair, clutching a bald-headed doll.

I'd worn my hair parted down the middle and twisted in two buns, one above each ear. It's how I keep it when I'm writing and little kids have been known to point when they see me and call me Mickey Mouse. Since the look seems to please them, I'd worn it that way especially for Mazie, thinking that having my long, bushy hair down might have put her off, and I stuck with the two buns until Baby Girl let me in on something.

We were getting on swell. She loved my 250-year-old writing studio, which had been the dairy cottage of the nearby chateau. It's got three bedrooms, one being a gallery that overlooks the living room on one side and leads to a terrace on the other. The house is surrounded by three acres with a small wood at the base of a steep slope of lawn. I try to keep it as tended as a park and to see her little legs running uphill and hear her yelling, 'Grammy, come!' was pure magic.

They'd been with me for a few days when Karis was on the phone talking to Jonathan one night and I wrapped Mazie up in my Kenyan mud cloth to take her for a stroll in the wheelbarrow under the August stars. There are only a hundred people in the village, so it's dead quiet, and that particular night, even the nearby farmer's guard dog had stopped his barking. The street lights were still on as we headed down the hill towards the cemetery, and Baby Girl was remarking on the bad smell of the neighbour's goat when out of the blue she switched the subject to say, 'Karis's mother has long, long hair.'

Kids. So who the hell was I, with my two buns?

I didn't ask. In fact, I just let the whole thing slide, because Baby Girl was still pretty new to me, and I thought it wasn't the right time to confuse her, seeing that she was already confused. I was remembering that in the various pictures of me around their house, my hair's down. I also thought maybe her father had been describing me before they caught the plane. Either way, I wanted her to know that I, Grammy, was also Karis's mother.

The following day after breakfast, she, Karis and I were heading off for a day's excursion to a bird sanctuary on the coast, and I slipped into the bathroom, slapped on some evening make-up and combed my hair down. It's such a different look from the buns, and I expected to surprise Mazie, but that moment she spotted me exceeded all expectations. It's seared upon my memory like a magic moment in a great movie.

I was in the drive off the front garden and having bent to stick something in the car, I rose just as she came rushing out of the house in my direction. She stopped short as she saw me, as if she'd seen an apparition. Her eyes widened and she seemed momentarily frozen to the spot as though she wasn't sure if it was Grammy with the buns or not. I'd swear that there had been a flash of pride and delight in her eyes as she turned on her heels and ran back into the house shouting, 'Mom! Mom! Come see! Grammy looks different! Come!' So of course I wore my hair down a few more times for her before they left for a week down at Mick's chateau.

When I waved her and Karis goodbye on the train, Baby Girl was clutching that bald-headed doll. So 5 months later, when Arnie Hill said that the chemo that I was to get after surgery would definitely make all my hair fall out, I figured that Mazie wouldn't have a problem with me being bald if she could see me making the transition from hair to hairless. The big question was how could I pull that off?

Son, you got to learn that in politics,
overnight chicken shit
can turn into chicken salad.

LYNDON B. JOHNSON

7

The Rolling Stones

Maybe you have to be an American who was alive and kicking in 1963 for the 22nd of November to be written large in your personal history. I was 16 that Friday when the message came over our high school Tannoy that President Kennedy had been shot. I was sitting in my French class at Oakland High, across the Bay Bridge from San Francisco. Kids ran home crying, and we didn't know he was dead yet. Kennedy's assassination in Texas changed all our lives. Not only because Vice President Lyndon Johnson, a Texan, took over the presidency but also because an American dream, however much of it was fantasy, was well and truly dead, never to be revived.

The following February, a foreign force known as The Beatles arrived in New York City. The white kids were wide open to these English invaders, who came sporting shaggy hair and electric guitars and a habit for Negro blues. Hot on the heels of The Beatles came bands like the Animals, Herman's Hermits and the Rolling Stones, as well as solo artists like Donovan and Tom Jones.

Undefeated

Whenever 22 November approaches, I always think back to that day in '63. Year after year, I can't help recalling how I sat at home alone in front of the TV waiting for my mother to come back from her government job as an accountant. Home was a two-bedroom apartment that she and I shared in Berkeley.

Jack Kennedy has been in Arlington Cemetery for 42 years, but his murder, and the way the suspect for his assassination was shot dead in front of the TV cameras, was the stuff of the TV shoot-'em-ups that I'd been consuming since nursery school. To see it happen for real was too shocking to erase from memory and on 21 November 2004, I was getting mental replays while boarding an Aer Lingus jet at Dublin airport.

My destination was Mick's chateau in France, where Keith and Charlie Watts were also staying, because the three of them were pulling their act together for a new Stones album and tour. When I'd spent the afternoon there five months earlier, Keith and Mick were already writing but Charlie was in London recovering from cancer. Though his cancer had been reported in the papers, I didn't know the details and resisted sending him and his wife, Shirley, a card. As much as I'd liked them both back in the old days, I hadn't seen them in years and figured they would be inundated with well-wishers.

Now I had my own dose of cancer. And since I knew that worrying was going to change nothing, I put it out of my mind and stayed focused on the book that had been my occupation for nearly five years. Whether it was Kennedy or Keith Richards, they had my focus only because Jimi's role in history was still my obsession. The '60s had been his decade, in the same way that it had been that of the Kennedys and a time when Britain's working class spawned a pop culture that affected the world.

74

I didn't care if Keith had agreed to talk to me because he thought I was dying. What mattered was that he was going to talk to me, and I needed to stay clear about what I needed answers to. I was neither going to take notes nor bring a tape recorder, because I think such things can put people off, and I wanted Keith to talk as freely as possible about that extraordinary period from '66 to '70.

Although I'd been involved with Mick in one way or another for 35 years, I'd made a point of never being in the same room with Keith until that summer of 2004, when we met for the first time at Mick's chateau. It had been the 60th anniversary of the D-Day landings in Normandy, and I suspected that the international hoo-ha that was being made of that was probably due to the invasion in Iraq. Even President George W. Bush had dared leave his homeland and was present in Normandy for the turnout.

By pure happenstance, that Sunday the 6th happened to coincide with France's Mother's Day and for all kinds of reasons, related to Mick making me a mother, it was peculiar enough that I should pass that afternoon with him. Keith was the surprise and Keith was the bonus.

His heroin addiction had been the reason that I'd avoided meeting him, but my attitude towards junkies did an about-turn in 1998 while I was the writer-in-residence at Mountjoy Prison. I was working with so many heroin addicts, teaching them to write about their lives, that I became their sponsor, and the book I put together of their work not only became a bestseller in Ireland but would have led to a career change had Alan, my partner at the time, not got cancer, because I'd begun to put together an organisation to examine heroin addiction.

So at Mick's back on D-Day, not only had I no longer been wary of meeting Keith, I even felt a certain affinity, believing that his addiction in the late '60s gave him an extra angle on Jimi, who had his own appetite for smack.

Though I knew that it had been sleazy of me to engineer an interview with Keith on the back of telling Mick that I had breast cancer, I figured I didn't have time for good manners. For all I knew, I was dying. Had killed my fool self for the sake of trying to write Jimi's short, tragic saga, believing as I did that it cast a new net over the context of modern history, world history and American history. And I was justly grateful for the bit of good luck that Keith was back at Mick's chateau that November as opposed to being in Connecticut with his American wife, Patty Hanson. Having had bands, I understood that since Keith was at the chateau to work, a couple of hours talking to me was an interruption.

When Mick told me that Keith had agreed, I'd been ecstatic. 'I'll be flying in from Dublin and can rent a car at Charles de Gaulle.'

'You don't want to do that. It's a long drive.'

'I don't mind. Really. It's three hours at most. No big deal.' Like I said earlier, my take on Jimi placed Keith so much at the vortex that I would've crawled there in order to talk to him about 1966, when his then girlfriend, Linda, engineered Jimi's entry into London's scene.

Mick insisted that he would have a car collect me at the airport. 'You don't need that drive,' he said.

I hated not being able to do for myself. Charity. Help. It struck me as weakness. But I was eight days away from going into hospital for major surgery. I knew it was only rational to conserve my strength for the removal of my right breast and the lymph glands under my right arm. It was time to learn to accept help graciously.

I like flying. Love that feeling of being above the world. But as we soared above the clouds on this flight, I was wondering whether it might be my last. Life. Death. Purpose. Being. Mind. Body. Soul. My thoughts dipped in and out of the Big Picture, and although I was unafraid of cancer, there have been so many stories of people dying while they're under the anaesthetic, that I was prepared to think that my tumour didn't have to be fatal for me to be nearing the end of my life.

Only seven days earlier, I'd flown into another Charles de Gaulle terminal from New York and gone straight on to a connecting flight to Dublin. Now I was back with knowledge about my body that was still so new that I had to run the word cancer around in my mouth like a marble to get used to the fact that it applied to me.

Whenever I fly into Paris, I head for my writing studio 70 miles to the north, so it was strange to disembark from the plane knowing that I wouldn't, and couldn't, see my few acres. The house, la montagne, which means the mount, is such a healing place, that my mind was telling me to overturn my plans and head there. It has a spirit all of its own and is more like a friend than a place.

I so respected that over the last 250 years it had survived winds and wars, had seen people and animals come and go, trees felled and trees grow. It had embraced me since 14 July 1989 when I took possession of it, and it took possession of me, indulging me in a gentle silence that I'd found nowhere else, so that even the noisy caws from the rooks in the nearby rookery couldn't disturb the power of its peace.

I've spent some of my happiest hours alone there. 'Hello, house,' I say on entering, whether I've been away for six months or a day. And five weeks earlier, when I was last there before my month in New York, I'd paused as usual before closing the door and took a good look around the living room saying, 'Thank you, little house, for being so good to me.'

It was in the bed there in the green room that I first felt the lump in my breast. It was walking along those lanes leading to the village that I'd decided the book I was working on was worth more than my life, and that decision was now, in November, going to be put to the test.

I knew that the D-Day lunch at Mick's chateau with him, Keith and their sound engineer, Pierre, was a sort of pivotal point in my life, because it was meeting Keith that afternoon which inspired me to begin the rewrite which I knew was the only way to display Jimi's life.

Keith struck me as wild. Not in an unseemly way but one I found appealing. Barefoot, his linen shirt open, his thinning hair wrapped in a red bandana, Navajo style, he'd bothered to drape neck, wrist and ankle in enough beads and bangles to look as weird as so many of us had dared to in our 20s. Of course, rock and roll power and wealth had afforded him this luxury, because it wasn't like he had to clock in for a job at a bank, but by contrast, Mick had been tamed, had knelt before Prince Charles to join the rank of knight. After 40 years of joint effort, theirs was a unique relationship which had either temporarily or permanently outlived their deep affection for each other.

I didn't expect a limo to be waiting for me at Charles de Gaulle airport, but I was surprised when the stranger holding up a card with my name took my small bag and led me to a blue van, explaining that he was a taxi driver. When he slid the door open for me, I noticed that he was nearly handsome. Not in that way that could get a girl into trouble, but his features were very neat, his dark wavy hair nicely cut, his sturdy build well ordered.

His taxi van was immaculately clean. Some would have been offended that Mick had sent a van to collect them but having room to stretch out on a back seat felt like a fabulous luxury. I was knackered, and after passing a few minutes of polite conversation with the driver, I knew that I'd soon be asleep.

There was something about curling up on the back seat of that van which took me back to my rock and roll days in the '60s and early '70s when I was out on the road singing with bands. Even as the band leader, I used to love to stick a boiled mint in my mouth and doze off with the sounds of boys yapping around me. Their talk of girls and music, sound equipment and hunger was so unenlightened and riveting. But that was history. I was now a grandmother, 58, and there was something unglamorous about me stretching out on the back seat of a van to conk out. But jet lag still had me in its clutches, and maybe the news of cancer and the long nights of alerting friends had me plain and simply worn out.

I don't know how long I slept, but on waking, as the van sped smoothly along the motorway, I noticed a fare meter ticking over near the driver's seat. Rubbing my eyes and trying to focus, I leaned forward and hoped that I was seeing things. The digits appeared to say that the fare was already 375 euros and we still had miles to go.

'That's the fare?' I asked the driver.

'Yes,' he replied.

I didn't know the French word for share and took a long-winded route to ask what could have taken half a second in English: 'Does Mr Jagger have a share in the taxi company?'

Now, imagine yourself in a van on a French motorway.

Imagine that prior to flying out of Dublin four hours earlier, you got sixty euros from a bank machine thinking that on a quick overnight trip to France that would be more than enough to get you home. I didn't dare ask whether I was expected to pay the fare, and assumed that, were that the case, the driver would have to accept my credit card, because what was his alternative?

My mind was going over my phone conversation with Mick, when he'd said that he'd send a car. Had I heard properly? Had I been listening? Had he said he'd send a taxi?

This is where my cancer kicked in. I decided that my life might be too short to waste any of it watching a fare meter rise. Instead, I settled back in my seat to watch the sun setting on the motorway and thought about the questions I hoped to ask Keith.

In the small, twelfth-century town of Amboise, a few miles from Mick's, as the van pulled up in front of tall gates, Mick's assistant, Dominic Faccini, was waiting with a smile. God was I glad to see him, knowing that if there was an altercation about paying the fare, Amboise was his turf and he could sort it out. Yet he's as much a Londoner as he is a Frenchman, and it strikes me as funny that he speaks both languages like a bit of a wide boy.

As he collected my bag and greeted the driver, I leapt out saying in a hushed tone, 'For fuck sake, the fare's nearly 500 euros. That's not right, is it?' He slid the van door closed and was pointing me towards the gate while I was still mouthing on. 'It's a scam of some kind, is it? I mean what lunatic would pay 500 euros to get from Charles de Gaulle . . . What's the deal?'

'You didn't pay, did you? Tell me you didn't,' said Dominic.

'My fucking return flight from Dublin cost a third of that!' My voice was rising as we walked from the street through a courtyard and up steps to the door of what appeared to be some sort of hotel that looked like it was closed for the season.

'Of course I didn't bloody pay it!' That he imagined I could have made me laugh. 'But nor do I want Mick to have to pay it. That's the craziest thing ever!'

'Don't worry about it,' Dominic said as he opened the front door. We took the stair, and on the second landing, he pointed to a door and said, 'That's where I am.'

'Whad'ya mean don't worry?' I ranted. My room for the night was another flight up. 'I'm not bloody worried. I'm furious. I could've rented a car for a tenth of that *and* had it to drive back to the airport tomorrow . . . You can be sure that I won't be heading back by taxi. There's a train. Karis took it from my place in August.'

I sometimes don't know when to shut up. Only while he was trying to unlock the door to my room did it occur to me that bitching to Mick's assistant about the free ride that his boss had provided was bad manners, even if Mick *was* getting ripped off. Half my problem was that I was tired. It had been a testy week both physically and mentally. In seven days, I'd checked out of midtown Manhattan, coped with the usual JFK madness, hung around half a day to fly from Charles de Gaulle to Dublin and on to Wicklow, with the stress of the cancer crap beginning two days later, not to mention my jet lag, and now here I was back in France. Pulling it all off with a couple of dimes and a credit card added to the tension, but then nobody had held a gun at my head and said I had to interview Keith.

There's nothing like a handsome, well-equipped, pristine hotel bathroom to restore my energy. And the one that came with my double bedroom had a generous supply of luxurious toiletries. I could've soaked and doused myself in various Damana orange blossom products all night, and while dozing off in the steamy bath I almost forgot why I'd come and wondered where I'd find the strength to pull my act together. Not only did my mass of hair need as much of a revamp as my make-up, I needed to rev up to face Keith.

Though I'd found him a pure joy five months earlier when we met on D-Day, this time around I wanted information from him about 1966 and the way his girlfriend at the time had turned Jimi's life around while Keith was on the road with the Stones. I knew that cancer was in my favour, because sympathy for my condition might encourage Keith to open up.

It was dark by the time I was saying hello to Mick, and I was rested enough by then to know not to mention the taxi fare. While we sat face to face in his living room making small talk, I was conscious of our daughter's picture sitting on the grand piano and tried to imagine Mazie romping in the room when they'd spent a week with Mick after the week with me in August.

But for the fact that Mick mentioned that Charlie Watts was there, I wouldn't have brought up the word cancer and intentionally made no reference to my own, because in the two days since my breast and lymph cancer had been confirmed, I noticed how uncomfortable it made people when I mentioned my condition.

Like Aids, cancer is a touchy subject.

'How's Charlie doing?' I asked.

'Fine,' said Mick. 'He'll be at dinner.'

I liked Charlie and his wife, Shirley. They'd been together longer than the band. I hadn't seen them for decades, not since the days when Mick was schmoozing me. 'Is he really going to do the tour?'

'Yeah.'

'Drumming's so strenuous.'

Men and health.

Over at the guest house, after Keith and I had been yapping and drinking for over an hour, he picked up his guitar. Sensing that he was on the verge of wanting a break, I asked if Charlie was upstairs. Though the main room on the floor above served as a rehearsal room and studio, adjoining it was a large bedroom. I was hoping I'd eventually find Charlie there, but when Mick's assistant came bounding down the stairs to head out the door, he told me that Charlie was over in the main house.

With the open fire crackling and the lights turned down low, Keith's quarters were so toasty that the thought of stepping out into the cold night air filled me with dread. 'You heading that way?'

'Yeah.'

'Can you tell Charlie I'm here, have breast cancer and would dearly love to talk to him?'

Keith stopped strumming and laid his guitar down. 'He can't tell him that. I'll go.'

Whoever's feelings Keith thought he was sparing when he headed out the door, I liked him for it.

The scar on Charlie Watts' slim neck wasn't the only indication that he'd recently had surgery for throat cancer. The softness of his voice had constraint, like he was taking extra care not to push it. He looked well, though, and his physique hadn't changed in the 30 years since I'd last seen him. It was obvious that under his sports jacket he was still thin and wiry, and he looked all the more well adjusted because he didn't dye his hair. It was short and, despite it being a pale grey, it was hard to believe that here was a granddad in his mid-60s. While he sat opposite me in Keith's, I remained cross-legged on the floor, sipping beer and grilling him with all the questions about cancer that people would soon be asking me. How did you find out you had it? What did they take out? Were you scared? What treatment have you had? How much more will you need? But the one question that I reserved, which is the one that makes cancer a scary word for people, was, 'Will you live?'

The clean thin surgical line across Charlie's throat reminded me of the razor cuts I used to see when I was a little kid in Philadelphia's ghetto. But had a razor slashed Charlie at that angle, he wouldn't have lived to tell the story. His wound was immaculate and totally healed, but well though he looked, I had to bite my tongue to keep from saying, 'Is it asking for trouble to go on tour?'

'My mastectomy's in eight days, and I guess I'll live,' I joked, as Keith, sipping vodka on the sofa, listened while gently plucking away at his guitar. Though he was a notorious rebel, with an enduring image as rock and roll's most drugged survivor, I nonetheless got the impression that the word cancer didn't pass easily from his lips.

There we were, three people in a room, with two of us affected by the disease. And still there was an element of timidity in speaking openly about it, as if the word itself was diseased. Yet cancer seemed to be reaching epidemic proportions for our generation. So many of us had it that it ceased to be the novelty it once had been, and for all our early rebelliousness, we '60s rebels, I felt a bit radical uttering the word with such ease, as if I was talking about ice cream.

Experience is not what happens to a man; it is what a man does with what happens to him.

ALDOUS HUXLEY

8

Comfort Zones

As much as I love Room 8 at the Bel Air, the confines of a hotel room were no place to hope to recover after major surgery. I knew I'd need a special space, a place of total privacy, free from observation, where I could fall apart if I needed to, smell bad without apology, look bad without caring, roam around at night, stare at the walls, talk to myself, receive company, or avoid company. But most importantly, be within shouting distance for help if ever I needed some, because I was going to be alone and knew I might find myself in more trouble at some point than I could handle.

No one would ever know how much Alan's cancer trip had prepped me for my own. It was a great boon that I'd already shared his experience in Dublin, where I was about to go through it all again but this time as my own advocate, my own carer. Knowing the territory, the city, the hospitals, what to ask, whom to ask, where to go, gave me confidence. I'd even spent mornings at ARC, the cancer support centre on Eccles Street, opposite the Mater Private Hospital, when Alan had been a patient.

I was very sure that I could take care of myself. Not cocky but merely that sort of secure that you feel when you're about to do something that you've handled well before, right down to the fact that no sooner than his cancer was diagnosed, I had to find us a new base near the hospital that was nice, convenient and affordable.

Now I had to use my skills to find a safe comfortable refuge for myself, but money was once again an issue and I was dreading having to tell Kevin Smullens at the Allied Irish Bank in Greystones that not only hadn't I sold my Jimi book yet but I also had cancer. Poor Kevin had endured years of me saying that I was nearly finished that book. Now he was going to have to endure my monologue about having breast cancer, because I believe there's no better place to go than the bank when you haven't got the rent.

When I went to the bank, Kevin was out, so I left him a note and with it a nappy-haired brown doll that I said he could send me when I was in hospital. Now I had to find myself somewhere to live.

The Freeman family who own and run the Bel Air are horse people. Their business is more focused on their equestrian centre than the small hotel. I loved flying in from somewhere to discover that Fidelma Freeman, the family matriarch and proprietress, was up to her elbows in arranging a show-jumping event or organising night rides for the Bel Air riding club. My life always seemed adventurous enough without riding a horse, but coming back on Thursday nights to find the riders in their old jodhpurs drinking Guinness at the hotel bar made me want to take up the sport. To hear Fidelma's tales about the horse she had during her pregnancy raised her even higher in my esteem, because I just couldn't imagine galloping around on horseback while I was pregnant. But she was special and proved herself to be even more so the morning that I decided to take her aside and explain that I had cancer and was scheduled for a mastectomy.

With Christmas coming, I wasn't sure whether it would be good for the hotel's business if people realised that there was a cancer patient staying there. The word cancer evokes such fear that people seem almost superstitious about it. I tried to imagine what it would be like for Fidelma having me on the premises while I was recovering. I remembered how I'd put myself in a hotel to recover after my hysterectomy, believing that I could get meals and service without burdening anyone. But that Folkestone hotel was much bigger than the Bel Air, where the phone system in the rooms doesn't always work and an old iron door bolt shuts us all in at night. I knew that people trooping in and out to visit me could be as much of a problem as members of the public hearing that I was upstairs recovering from a mastectomy. It seemed only fair to ask Fidelma if she'd mind if I stayed on.

'Mind if we have a chat?' I whispered after having my breakfast in the dining room. There wasn't a soul in reception that morning, because there were few hotel guests in late November, but the Freemans and their small staff were already revving up for the various parties being catered there over the Christmas holidays.

'Let's talk in here,' Fidelma said, pointing to the living-room salon.

Her parents bought the Bel Air when she was five, and they also had Dalkey Castle, a hotel closer to town, so Fidelma had personal stories going back half a century about the Bel Air, its ghosts and its guests. To come in on a cold winter's night and share a pot of tea with her, munch some hot apple pie and listen to her peel off ghost stories was one of the advantages of having the Bel Air as my Irish base. And my favourite of the public rooms was the living-room salon. It was directly below Room 8, where I was staying, and, despite the chill, the room was washed in sunlight that was streaming in through the tall windows overlooking the meadow.

Fidelma's short hair looked like she had just blown it dry and she was neat in a navy skirt and blouse as we stood face to face at the window with the morning sun warming our shoulders: two tough old broads being ladylike.

'Would you like tea, Marsha?'

'Fidelma, I know you're busy,' I began.

'Never too busy for you,' she smiled. She always made me feel that I was as special as to her as one of her beloved old oil paintings.

'I won't beat around the bush,' I said, shifting my eyes from hers. 'I've got cancer,'

Though I'd declared my illness to people many times on the phone, she was the first I told face to face, and I was surprised that the pronouncement left a tightness in my throat.

'Where?'

'Breast. Lymphs. My op is on the 30th at St Vincent's Private. I'll be in for ten days. With Christmas coming, having me upstairs will be the last thing you need, because for all I know, I may still be unable to move around much.'

Fidelma's a sort of female Clint Eastwood. Not that she looks like him, but she has that sort of straight, no bullshit manner of a Dirty Harry. Half the reason I stay at the Bel Air is that Fidelma is the best of Ireland. That morning, she didn't waiver or falter and was so quick in with, 'We'll manage. And you'll be fine. Cancer's nothing these days,' that I wanted to hug her. But, of course, there was no guarantee that I'd be fine. Operations can produce complications. I had to keep that in mind.

'I'm thinking about all the coming and going.'

When she offered to show me a chalet, I was tempted to decline, thinking of the money. Something else said take a look.

I was wearing a leather jacket, Fidelma was in a sweater, and the November wind was blowing my hair in my face as we made our way up the steep grade past some horse boxes and the sign that says 'Holiday Village'. Fallen leaves crunched underfoot and grey clouds promised some afternoon showers as I looked skywards at the craggy hilltop that overlooks the grounds of the Bel Air's riding arena and old stone outhouses. The woodsy atmosphere at that back side of the Freemans' property is so different from the tended lawns and flower beds near the hotel entrance.

'Willy's just there in Number 1,' Fidelma was saying as she fiddled to open the door to Number 3. Willy, who's twenty-four, is the youngest of her four adult children. Like his three sisters, he works at the hotel. And like their mother and father, Bill, the younger Freemans have the air of hard-working country folk rather than lords and ladies of the manor. Seeing the daughters clomp about in their muddy boots from the stables, no one would imagine that they were heirs to these extensive lands, with the stables and 60 well-groomed horses, all in the beautiful Wicklow county known as the garden of Ireland.

The two red sofas sold me on Number 3 even before I laid eyes on the immaculate country kitchen, which had two glass doors leading to a large deck. The back of the hotel was visible from there and one of the two double bedrooms upstairs had a still better view towards the hills and the Irish Sea out towards Newcastle. A host of 20 crows perched on a phone line squawked back and forth as I gazed out from what I was crossing my fingers and hoping would be home when I came out of hospital.

I'll never know if she made the price right, or if the price happened to be right, but one minute I had a housing problem, and the next I had the key to Number 3.

The chalet was perfect for my needs. All I had to do was hang pictures of my own. The décor throughout was bright, but not too bright. I was close to the Bel Air but not too close, and with Willy only two doors away, I felt that if ever I got into trouble late at night, I had easy access to an able body who knew me. The house lacked nothing but a phone, and until Fidelma got one installed, my mobile would do. With enough bedrooms to accommodate visitors, all I needed to worry about was the rent.

'Do you want help moving your bags over?' Fidelma asked.

I'd already moved in that afternoon when I drove to the Blackrock Clinic for the full CAT scan which Arnie Hill had ordered. And I was glad that I had Number 3 to come back to afterwards because of what happened during the CAT scan.

While the slim, blonde radiographer told me how to position myself on the screen, she asked me a bit about my life and revealed enough about hers to let me know that I was in able hands. She was relaxed and chatting away as she studied a screen that highlighted the bones in my body. We were laughing about something when suddenly she went quiet. I couldn't see her face, because I was lying on my back in a big cylinder.

'What's up?' I asked, trying to keep the same easy tone in which we'd been chatting.

She didn't answer fast enough for my liking. When she finally said, 'Have you had a collar bone injury?' though I was still on my back, I was dying to sit up.

'No . . . I have not had a collar bone injury,' I said. 'Why do you ask?'

As I spoke, my mind went racing through my past trying to come up with a collar bone injury. I couldn't recall any injury.

'Maybe a bad fall?'

'No . . .'

'Oh,' she said, in a voice that now sounded too serious.

'What's up? What do you see?'

'There's a hot spot here.'

A hot spot?

Christ! A fucking hot spot! Though I had no idea what a hot spot was, the radiographer's voice was telling me that it wasn't a good thing to have. Since the cancer in my breast tumour had spread into some lymph nodes, was I now about to discover that it had metastasised into my bones?

When my close friend, Mary Ove, died from bone cancer in 1993, I recalled her daughter, Indra, telling me about how much pain Mary had been in. I was still thinking about the cancer in Mary's lower spine while I was building a peat briquette fire in the iron stove in the living room at Number 3. Driving back from the Blackrock Clinic, after the blonde radiographer had taken another scan of my shoulder, I had dropped into the supermarket and bought food, candles and a bottle of port. I knew alcohol was no good for me with cancer, but I needed something to slow me down.

It would be wrong to say that I wanted to relax. Quite the

opposite. I was setting myself up for some positive thinking. I knew I needed a hint of drunkenness for clarity.

The two red sofas were identical. One sat between the two windows which looked onto a small embankment of bushes. The other faced the fire and was destined to become my perch. It was against the wall. The pine coffee table in front of it was bound to become my workplace, as would the long, refectory kitchen table. The decor was so different from the hotel, the charm of which rested on the fact that the Victorian building with its sweeping mahogany staircase was what you might call shabby chic: though everything seemed to work together, nothing quite matched. The chalets, on the other hand, were only a couple of years old. Even the fluffy towels matched the rusty-red duvet covers, which went well with the red riding outfits of the hunters illustrated in the large framed pictures on the walls and the heavy beige drapes at the windows.

Having shifted all my things there before my appointment at the Blackrock, I now had no reason to pop over to the hotel, but the chalet's newness made it less than the ideal place to reflect upon what had happened during the CAT scan.

'Fucking bone cancer. Lord have murgatory,' I laughed to myself as I poured myself some port and hunkered down cross-legged, Native American style, on the floor in front of the orange flames of the peat fire. To the quietness of the night, I'd added the magic of candlelight.

I'm not a drinker, so it was only going to take half a small wine glass of port to get me drowsy. Not tipsy but just woozy enough for some creative thinking. Some of my friends smoke a bit of grass to get to that state of mind. A bit of port will do it for me, and before I drained the last ounce, I'd curled up by the roaring fire to sleep.

My life wasn't all drama. Sprawled either side of the noteworthy bits, like me taking Fidelma aside that morning to tell her about my cancer and hearing the radiographer say the words 'hot spot', I had time-consuming everyday stuff to do, such as packing my clothes to move them from the hotel to the chalet, where they had to be unpacked; my hour's drive to the Blackrock and hanging around for my CAT scan, followed by shopping at a busy Dublin supermarket. However grateful I was for the eggs, bacon, milk, bread, tea, coffee and marmalade that Fidelma put in the small chalet fridge for me, I needed to stock the place for my return from a ten-day hospital stay. Especially if I had bone cancer, I needed to leave nothing undone.

The thought of dying didn't bother me. I think of myself as I do others: we're all just pilgrims passing through. We've all come to die. Maybe this is our purpose in living. Death. Why fear this equalising factor that Nature affords each of us? I figure that we'll go with all we were born with, that indefinable something called soul.

Night after night, that week before my surgery, it was both restful and restorative to light a few candles and sit with a small glass of port by the open peat fire. I wanted to have no regrets about losing a breast or my hair, and to achieve that I needed the quiet time alone to prepare for the physical change that was about to happen. I was happy to distance myself from others, because it seemed that, without exception, my attitude differed from that of everyone else. When I told someone that I was going to have a mastectomy and chemotherapy, they felt sorry for me.

'There's nothing to be sorry about,' I repeated more times than I cared to count. Having one breast would be different but no more than that – simply different. It couldn't diminish me, and as long as my granddaughter wasn't confused by me being bald, I didn't give two hoots about what anybody else thought.

My 15 years in the rock and roll business was about to hold me in good stead, because musicians, including me, went out of our way to look different. It was called having an image. Now cancer was about to create a new look for me.

When I rang my TV producer friend, Stuart Prebble, to ask if he thought that there might be a documentary to be made of my cancer trip, he was hesitant.

'My attitude's so different to anyone that I've spoken to, that I wanted to share it. Why's it such a big deal about losing my breast? What's worrying is that people place too much importance on tits! And how's that happened?'

Though Stuart's highly intelligent and not short on opinions, he's pensive and, rather than jump at my idea, he said, in that bassy voice of his which sounds like he should be doing movie commercials, 'Let me have a think about it.'

His success with *Grumpy Old Men*, the BBC series he produced, overshadowed his first love and talent as a documentary film-maker. Not only was he the commissioning editor for the documentary Alan had directed with me in Philadelphia, which is what brought Alan and me together and brought me to Ireland, but Stuart's work on my Jimi book was the greatest support that I got. The notion to ring him came after I had downed some port and fallen asleep by the peat fire.

The nightly comfort of those flames and that port were inspiring. It was also thanks to them that I remembered that during the summer of 2003 in France, as I turned to wave to a neighbour while flying down the hill on my bike, I went over the handlebars, badly scraping my right elbow. I could easily have damaged my right collar bone at the same time, and on relating this accident to the doctor who was assessing the additional X-rays I'd been asked to have on my hot spot, he sounded as relieved as I felt.

'Good,' he said. 'That explains it.'

So it was back to just worrying about the rent. I ticked bone cancer off the list.

It's never too late to be what you might have been.

GEORGE ELIOT

9

Room with a View

From the distance, it was clear that he was wearing a black leather coat and had a healthy head of curly grey hair. As I watched him approach, I waved and was thinking, 'Trust Stuart Prebble to send me a cute director.'

'Eamon. Eamon. Eamon. Why's that so hard to remember? Eamon.' I'd been repeating his name to myself ever since he'd rung from the Bel Air reception to say that he'd arrived from England and was going to stroll over to the chalet to say hello. My brain was a sieve that Sunday, 28 November. Eamon O'Connor. Eamon O'Connor. Eamon O'Connor . . .

Despite his grey hair, as he got closer, I could see that he was probably in his late 30s. Early 40s at most. His round, intelligent face was kind. What gave it sex appeal was the small beard around his mouth. Before he smiled back and said hello, I stuck out my hand to shake his. What makes you instantly know that you'll have a rapport with somebody? Is it their looks, their clothes, the glint in their eye, their aura? The minute I shook Eamon's hand, I knew that I'd met a new friend.

His accent bent towards English, but there was more than a hint of Irish and I learned that he was Belfast born and bred, but Northern Ireland was still foreign to me.

That Sunday had been wet. Ashford's late-afternoon sky was grey and dreary, and I was anxious to get in out of the cold, damp air, because, were I to catch a cold, my mastectomy would have been postponed. Karis's pregnancy was in the forefront of my mind and it was paramount that I get my surgery behind me for her sake.

Although it was Eamon O'Connor I was meeting, in spirit I saw him as my buddy Stuart Prebble and his lovely wife, Marilyn. Stuart is no average TV executive, and Marilyn, who I call Marzipan, is no average wife. The way they'd dealt with losing a teenage daughter to cystic fibrosis in 1996 wasn't the only thing that had won my respect and trust. It was also those two years that Stuart had worked unpaid as an editor on the Jimi book while setting up his TV production company. Time and again, he'd proven that his patience and love of truth was boundless. So, as much as Eamon arrived as Stuart's director, so Stuart was Eamon's representative in my mind. I trusted Stuart wholeheartedly and believed that nothing would wind up on the screen which I hadn't approved. At that stage, we were all working on spec.

If we could pull off a documentary about my breast cancer and the journey into this dark and deadly territory that I was about to make, then I felt that nothing of my experience would be a waste, because at least some viewers were bound to benefit. What I didn't realise was how many dire moments would be transformed into busy events by the mere fact that a television crew would be on hand to record them. By the same token, however, with a crew in tow, I was about to be deprived of the solitude that my soul was sometimes destined to need during the uphill struggle ahead. Fortunately, the day before my surgery at St Vincent's Private Hospital turned out not to be one of these days.

Since I wasn't due to check into the hospital until late afternoon on Monday, 29 November, I had seen no harm in going to my friend Clodagh's 50th birthday party on the 27th. In fact, I saw her big Saturday night sit-down dinner as remedial, since the option would have been to sit at home alone with too much time to think. Thinking about what was going to happen could achieve nothing but instil worry and fear. The antidote that weekend was to stay busy and avoid being alone, which was made easy by my friend Kathy Gilfillan and her husband, Paul McGuinness. They'd invited me to join them and friends for a big Saturday lunch, and since they were also going to Clodagh's 50th birthday dinner, they suggested that, rather than driving back to Ashford from their estate in Annamoe, I go with them. With hindsight, I see that day as the beginning of Kathy and Paul looking out for me, extending their generosity in ways too extraordinary to pause here and mention.

Since I was promoting one book and working on another when I moved to Ireland in 1995 to be with Alan, I kept to myself and was slow in making friends. Kathy was my first. Her husband, Paul McGuinness, as U2's manager, was on a world tour with the band. Kathy had more free time than usual and was interested in turning *Repossessing Ernestine*, my book about my grandmother, into a screenplay. She's since become a joint owner of a small Irish publishing imprint and has her hands full commissioning books and seeing them through publication. Paul's business is managing Bono and U2, and as head of Principle Management, his other interests also keep him jetting around the world. They're a rare rock and roll couple: solid and steady and devoted to their two kids, Alexandra and Max. And my special relationship with Max enhanced my friendship with his parents.

He was 17 at the time, a bit cantankerous and as much of a loner as I am when he decided to travel across France by himself in 2003 taking photographs. The highlight of my summer was his five days with me at my writing studio. Not many kids can cope without TV and video, and he managed painlessly. His insistence on doing the dishes, penchant for a fireside argument and willingness to tramp around First World War sights with me were just a few of the things that warmed me to Max, but I wasn't sure what warmed him enough to me to ask for a return visit in October 2004. By the time I waved him off, he knew me better than most, had seen the solitary side of my existence that few people ever witness. So when Karis insisted that I have someone at the hospital with me during my surgery, I asked Kathy if I could ask Max.

This conversation took place over Saturday lunch while we had hours to kill before leaving for Clodagh's birthday dinner. Kathy had taken me up to one of the guest bedrooms, because I'd said it might be wise for me to nap before the party. What I was really angling for was silence. Writing for the past 20 years has afforded me great doses of it, and I'm as addicted to it as others are to music.

Kathy has a gentle disposition and rarely swears, so she didn't say, 'Have you lost your fucking mind. Of course you can't ask my 18 year old to babysit your surgery!' No, Kathy, always the lady, merely looked away and said, 'I'll do it.'

'To be honest,' I said, 'I'd rather no one did it. But Karis insists, and if it'll make her feel better, I have to go along with it. But surgery could take hours, Kathy, and my surgeon has scheduled me to be in theatre from 8.30 on Tuesday.'

When she said, 'I haven't anything on,' I was willing to bet that she was going to have to cancel something. Apart from her publishing interests, she's on several boards and does a lot of charity work, like the edition of *Peter and the Wolf*, illustrated by Bono, which she'd been putting together for a Christie's auction and Christmas sales.

The guestroom was on the second floor overlooking the grounds of the estate, which stretched further than my eye could see when I stood looking from the window before slipping between the crisp white sheets of the single bed and wondering what I'd done to deserve such good friends as the McGuinnesses.

When Kathy and I first met in '96, I was living with Alan in a woodsy corner of Roundwood, a small hilltop village in the Wicklow Mountains, which was only a ten-minute drive from Paul and Kathy's place. Though our mutual passion for walking and books was our common ground, the fact that she was such a devoted mum was what really attracted me to her. Money and the rock world gave Kathy endless opportunities to shirk parenting, and the fact that she insisted on driving Max to school and was always there for Alexandra impressed me.

Yet as much as I'd grown to love her and her family over the years, lying in bed in the guestroom late that Saturday afternoon, it made me uncomfortable to think that, on my behalf, poor Kathy was going to have to waste a whole morning hanging around St Vincent's Private Hospital on Tuesday so that Karis would have somebody to ring while I was under the knife. Call it pride but I hate asking favours. Now, with cancer, it was something that I was going to have to learn to tolerate.

That Saturday night, it teemed with rain when Paul and Kathy's driver, Kevin, drove us to Clodagh and her twin sister's

50th birthday dinner. I intended to slip off very early, because Eamon O'Connor was coming to meet me at the chalet the following day, to discuss the possibility of filming my cancer trip. What I didn't know was that it was a sit-down affair for a hundred people, and to leave the table in the middle of the meal was impossible. When I did find the right moment to slip over to Paul and say that I really had to leave, I was reeling with exhaustion.

Leaning forward to give me a goodbye kiss, he said, 'You're about to have a rough ride. You'll need help.'

'Nothing to it,' I said. 'Piece of cake.'

Why did everybody assume that having my breast removed was going to be such a big deal? I didn't get it. But soon I would.

I'd resisted having Internet access for all kinds of reasons, the main one being that when I was working at la montagne, I wanted my laptop to remain a sacred work space. I liked getting letters and sending them. Liked touching a piece of stationery knowing that it had been touched by a friend, with the handwriting being as distinctive and important to me as his or her voice. Making cards to send to friends was my favourite pastime, and I saw e-mail as the McDonald's of personal correspondence. Too quick, too easy, too samey and superficial. Yet I had to admit that in hospital, e-mail would be the ideal way to stay in touch with family and friends. I remembered that when Alan was in hospital, the most tiring thing for me was answering calls from people enquiring about his progress. Day after day, day in and day out, I'd sometimes want to scream or cry seeing how many calls had come in on our answering machine. Facing my own spell in hospital, and realising that I'd be the only person to take calls, I knew it was crucial to find a deterrent. E-mail seemed to be the answer, but I wondered if Internet access was possible in hospital.

I was sitting in the kitchen of Kathy and Paul's Dublin townhouse, when she told me about the little handheld wireless e-mailing device that required no phone line. Be it fashion, books or technology, she's up on the latest. 'It's called a BlackBerry. Haven't you heard of them?' she asked with that faint accent of hers that makes me forget that she's from the north. 'There's a shop that sells them on Baggett Street. Near the corner. Opposite Tesco.'

I was almost out the front door before she finished the sentence, because it was Monday and time was running short. When the salesman told me the hefty price, I reached for my credit card. The 350 euros was far more than I could afford, but measured against how much money and energy it could save me in hospital phone calls, 350 was cheap. When I walked out of the O$_2$ store with that little BlackBerry, I could never have guessed how it was going to change my life.

Film crews seem oblivious to boundaries. Eamon O'Connor and his were no different. On Monday afternoon, while they were filming me unloading my bags from the boot of the car to walk into St Vincent's, they seemed oblivious to the security guard in the parking lot who was giving us the evil eye because the car and van we'd arrived in were almost blocking the entrance. The last thing I needed was a to-do with the security guard before registering for my ten-day stay in this small Dublin hospital.

He wasn't the only person eyeing us. Being late afternoon but still light out, there were patients in the glassed entrance who were staring at us, too. I've filmed enough over the years to be used to the public's curiosity, and having previously worked on three documentaries about myself, this was known territory. What was different and made me self-conscious and uncomfortable is that I was about to become an in-patient with my life on the line. I wanted no one at the hospital, not even the uniformed guard in the parking area, to have it in for me. Still, I'd proposed doing this documentary and knew how relevant it was to let Eamon shoot me entering the hospital for the first time.

What this minor mental conflict served to do was take my mind off what was actually happening; I was too preoccupied with filming and its consequences to be nervous about the fact that I was here to have my breast and the lymph glands under my arm removed the following morning. Did my hair look all right? Was my forehead shining? Was there lint on my skirt? How were my tights? No runs or sags at the knees?

I was in the bizarre position of being alone yet not alone. Having arrived with three able-bodied men, I didn't have to carry my bag upstairs, but the fact that they were strangers added to the surreal nature of the situation in which I found myself: an African-American was registering alone into a small, private Dublin hospital while a director from Manchester and a small crew hired for the day shoot some footage of her arrival.

One might say that it was just bad luck that my blood samples were taken in a ground-floor room with a large window overlooking the parking lot. I tried not to notice the cameras aimed in our direction. This intrusion and snooping was going to be part of my life throughout my stay in St Vincent's Private Hospital.

I was delighted with the spacious ground-floor room and bath that I was allocated. The moment I spotted the built-in dressing table that I could use as a desk, I was itching to unpack my books and my laptop. A nest of flowers from my close friend Dana Wynter, which had arrived before I did, were sitting on the sill of the big picture window that took up the far wall and overlooked an immaculate golf course. From the hospital bed, facing south, I was going to have a great view of green grass and tall palms and a perfect, uninterrupted skyline. There wasn't a building in sight. Natural light flooded the room, which felt tucked away and slightly isolated, though it was only 20 paces from the nurses' station. I was raring to throw a few bits and pieces around, to convert it from an impersonal hospital room and make it as much home as healing place.

While the nursing registrar was showing me how the bedside phone and lights worked, adding that, after a light supper, I'd be fasting, I was conscious that Eamon and the film crew still had a bit of work to do before I'd be left alone. I needed to think and prepare, like one would getting ready for a performance. I needed to find my centre and my calm. Needed to empower myself with a sense of what was, what had been and what would be, so that I was my own surgeon, reducing the actual removal of my breast to a mere formality.

The myth of the Amazons appealed to me. (Or is it factual that thousands of years ago there was a great tribe of warring women who amputated their right breast to make them better able to handle the javelin and bow and arrow? Their left breast remained to nurse their children, and their husbands remained at home.) Since I love coincidence, I got a lot of satisfaction from the fact that at the National Theatre in 1983 I'd played Hippolyta, queen of the Amazons, who marries Theseus in Shakespeare's comic love story, *Midsummer Night's Dream*. Now, here I was in Ireland, about to become an Amazon for real.

Sleep came quickly that night, after I'd sent a few e-mails on my new BlackBerry and made a few phone calls, and when I awoke at 3 a.m. as usual, oddly the hospital room didn't feel alien. I felt I was where I was supposed to be.

Having left the curtains open and the window slightly open, there was enough cold night air seeping into the room to make the warm bed feel all the more cosy. It was glorious to lie there watching the stars, as dreamy thoughts filled my head.

I thought about my good friend Pea, from my college days at Berkeley. She'd had her mastectomy 14 months earlier at the Sloane Kettering in New York without me knowing. Now it was my turn, and being only hours away from surgery, I felt good about having gotten myself so quickly to the cut once I'd been diagnosed. It also felt good to be in situ. In hospital, fasting and ready.

Work wise, with Keith's interview in the bag, there was nobody left that I needed to talk to about Jimi. And some of what Keith had said had been so illuminating that I figured it was worth losing a breast if that's what it took to get that interview.

Now all I had to do was finish the doggone book . . .

My circumstances that 29 November seemed so straightforward. I knew that I'd either be fine or I'd die, and the possibility of the latter still didn't bother me. Having always seen myself as a pilgrim passing through life, if cancer was destined to kill me, I had no problem about that. Whatever was going to happen would happen. I lay there thinking about Arnie Hill, trying to imagine his home life and how he managed to have such a demanding career with four small boys at home. It was important to remember that he was just another human being doing a job, and I hoped that he was having a good sleep and would start the day ready for it: neither worried nor tired, neither harried nor vexed.

Surgery was scheduled for 8.30 a.m. on Tuesday. I'd been fasting since the previous night and awake since dawn. Somehow, it didn't feel right to be going under an anaesthetic while a crew about whom I knew nothing sliced into me. Who were they? How many would there be? I was thinking about them rising that day to come to work, and for them it was just another day's work, another stranger needing help. It must have felt like a terrible burden some days, and I was trying to think of what I could do to lighten it. So, deciding that I should give Arnie and his surgical team a laugh, I grabbed a pen from a mug of them that I had on my bedside cupboard, and started to draw a message to them on my breast. I used a coloured pen, and, although it wasn't easy writing upside down, I had a devilish good time printing, 'Thanks for your help. Enjoy!'

Karis wasn't surprised to hear that I'd been up to devilment, and having a laugh about my prank took the edge off what a mother and daughter would say to each other in such circumstances. It was nearly midnight her time when we spoke. She knows me so well and knows that sympathy is the last thing I want or need when things are tough. Had anybody heard our upbeat conversation, they might have imagined that I was about to head off on a summer holiday. I assured her that I was fine. 'Take care of yourself, kiss Mazie, and you know better than to worry about me . . . I'm fine. Kathy Gilfillan will be here soon and will give you a ring if anything goes down.'

When Kathy arrived, I looked like any normal patient, and though I mentioned the drawing on my breast, I didn't show her. It was still my breast, and so there remained the fact that it was still a private spot.

'It's so good of you to come,' I told her, embarrassed that she was putting herself out so much for my benefit. 'Trust you to be early. And please don't feel that you have to hang around here the whole time.' She'd risen in November's dark, and it was still barely light out.

'I've got stuff to read,' said Kathy. She was wearing her brown coat with the fur collar and very little make-up. She seemed calm and did just the right amount of talking before they came to slip me onto a gurney and roll me down to the theatre.

Five years earlier, when Alan was having his surgery, I insisted on sitting outside the door of the theatre and tried not to look anxious, reading a book but barely able to take in the words. When his surgeon, Ronan O'Connell, came out once, he walked over and said, 'It could be a while. Go for a coffee.' But I dared not leave that spot, because I'd asked all my friends who'd crossed over to the spirit world, to hang on in there with Alan. And if I left, maybe they would, so I stayed. That scene of me sitting alone on a bench outside the theatre was replaying in my mind as the nurse slipped a cap over my hair and said that I'd first feel just a bit sleepy after the jab.

'Do feel free to pop out,' I urged Kathy as the two hospital porters were about to roll me to the elevator. 'And beware that I might say something ridiculous when you next see me . . . When I had my hysterectomy, coming down off the anaesthetic had me so crazy that I was yelling that the nurses were trying to kill me and insisted on calling Hugh Quarshie, this actor friend who I had a crush on, and making him read to me on the telephone, because his voice is soothing. Crazy I was. Totally fucking out of my mind.'

That was the last thing I remembered saying to her and it seemed that one minute I was staring at the ceiling outside of the operating theatre and the next I was opening my eyes to find I was back in my hospital room holding her hand.

Kathy was seated on my right. On the side where I'd been cut. Her expression as always was calm. No hint of panic or fear or sympathy. I knew that I could depend upon her not to over-dramatise the situation. She always strikes me as being more Scots than Irish. Utterly rational and practical. Some say it's because she's Protestant and from the north, and while I used to reject such assessments as purely prejudice, the longer I'd been in the Republic, the more I saw the truth in it. I thought I was smiling at Kathy, but I was still so overwhelmed by the anaesthetic that I wasn't sure. She held my hand and I dozed in and out with daylight pouring into the room. I didn't know how long I'd been gone nor that it was nearly noon.

My cotton hospital gown, tied at the neck, was slightly bloody. Nothing hurt, but my mouth was dry, and on my right side where my breast had been, there was a long slit running across my chest that was sewn together with black stitches. Halfway between my right underarm and waist, two long thin tubes were attached to my side and fluid from my fresh wounds was draining into two pint-size plastic bottles. Having already dealt psychologically with my amputation on the days preceding surgery, I was relieved that the job was done. No more anticipation. The new me was alive, intact and at least I hadn't become one of those horror stories about patients who die under anaesthetic.

'Hi, Kathy. Aren't you good . . .'

'You've got a couple of Fed-Exs, Marsha,' she said softly.

'Will you open them?' I wasn't yet able to sit up. But with my head propped up in a mound of four pillows in starched white cases, I could see easily around my hospital room. My books, my laptop, my new little BlackBerry and Kathy.

She opened the Fed-Ex in a flat envelope first. 'It's a letter.'

'From whom?'

'Keith.'

I smiled. It had been a week since I'd sat with him at Mick's. That he'd written was as much of a surprise as his astute insights and his memory, which I'd expected to be shaky due to his drug history.

Had Kathy been anyone else, I would never have let her read his letter, because whatever he said was private. But I longed to know and knew I could trust her.

'Dear Bunny,' she began, with her voice hardly above a whisper. It was the sweetest letter, which he'd signed, 'one love, Keith'. I couldn't have asked for better from anybody at that moment. His kind sentiments about me as a woman, as a person and his reference to our talk about Jimi were so perfect for me at that moment, and it was simply a well-timed coincidence that, although he'd written it days earlier, it reached me there on 30 November when my breast had just been amputated.

I liked him so much, respected him and was glad that he felt the same about me.

The second Fed-Ex was a much bigger parcel and was from Karis.

Along with the small framed pictures of her and Mazie, she'd sent a beautiful silk shawl and a bowl that Mazie had made. But the touching surprise was that she'd also sent the expensive suede slippers that Jonathan had spoiled her with some years ago. They were beautifully made and so comfortable that whenever I visited her in LA, I loved sneaking a little wear of them, and would ask, like a kid asking her mother, 'Can I have a little wear of your slippers?'

To hold them in my hand, Karis's two brown suede slippers, slightly worn and shaped by her feet, carried more memories than at that moment I could handle in my woozy, postoperative state. But to cry in front of Kathy would have been an unforgivable breach of our ungirlish friendship, so I waited until after she'd help me ring Karis and was gone.

A view from my window can become as vital to me as a trusted friend, and since I had to be in a hospital bed, I couldn't have wished for a bigger window and a prettier scene in central Dublin. The tall palms made me feel that I wasn't far from California, as did the emerald-green golf course, especially when the sun would occasionally break through the Dublin sky while I dozed on and off that afternoon. E-mails and sensational flowers kept arriving, and when it was late enough to ring my daughter again, I did.

'I'm glad that you made me have somebody here. Kathy was just perfect. She couldn't have been better. And your slippers, Miss Karis. They're the best. Really inspired it was of you to send them. And can you believe that I've had the sweetest letter from Keith Richards?'

Her slippers were under my bed. His letter was under my pillow.

As night fell, I could see the sun going down. The colours, so pink, fading to peach and apricot, were beautiful. With the door to my room closed, I had that silence that serves me so well. Yep, I had everything I needed, apart from my right breast.

II

Down for the Count

He allowed himself to be swayed by his conviction that human beings are not born once and for all on the day their mothers give birth to them, but that life obliges them over and over again to give birth to themselves.

GABRIEL GARCÍA MÁRQUEZ

10

Amazon

A nurse had been in several times throughout the night to check on me, but that Wednesday morning, the day after surgery, as I lay in bed gathering my thoughts with a clearness that I lacked the day before, the hospital day had not begun. There was a stillness. A silence. Nothing stirred but my mind, which was now busy deciding how I would proceed since I hadn't died. With my chest stitched and bandaged, the two tubes in my right side draining into two clear plastic bottles and the intravenous drips in my left arm, my movements were restricted but not my thoughts.

Sometimes I see illness as a time for letting go. I can get the flu and succumb to it. Loll in bed under a mound of duvets, pampering myself with cups of tea and hot toddies, bowls of soup and good books, letting my body rest and recover. Being a workaholic, I think that flu can sometimes be a good thing, a time when my body is forced to pause, to stop and rest. But at other times, illness is war, and there can be no surrender: I know I must fight to recover my strength, my control, never allowing my Self to be overtaken by sickness. So on the first day of December 2004, a Wednesday, when

I woke in that hospital bed, with my right breast and the lymph glands under my right arm gone, I knew it wasn't the time to enjoy being served. It was a fighting time. No surrender.

If I allowed myself to succumb to pain, discomfort or the comforts of being in hospital, I was sunk. I sensed that in some way surgery had been as much a trauma for my body as a knife attack and that I had to fight to regain my balance, to recover my strength and empower my mind over my body. If I stayed strong in mind, I could resist feeling sick. If I stayed strong in heart, I could resist self-pity. If I stayed strong in body, the cut I'd had the day before was no more than a slash that would take time to heal. Lying in that hospital bed, propped up on the mound of pillows, eager for daylight, I was reminding myself that I hadn't been mortally wounded and must not act that part. So what part was I going to play? Deciding my role would make scripting it easier. I definitely wasn't going for the sick role or the poor me role or the superman role. I wasn't sick. I'd felt way worse with a bad head cold. Since I hadn't been rendered deaf, blind or cripple, I had no right to play 'poor me'. But nor was I to pretend nothing had happened. Cancer can be terminal. Maybe I was dying, so I wasn't to try to lift any tall buildings from my hospital bed. There's a difference between inner strength and a show of strength.

I felt in no way diminished by having one breast. This was the new me. My new body shape and a new beginning. I held to the notion of the Amazons. There was strength in that for me, but who was this tribe and why had they chosen what cancer had chosen for me? A single breast. I'd asked various friends to get me info about the single-breasted Amazons, but even before it arrived, I had in my head an image of these female warriors. Thinking about them brought to mind what my stepfather, Allison, had told me in 1999, when he was no longer officially my stepfather because my mother, whom we called Ikey, had divorced him. After 25 years of marriage, they parted in their 70s in a long and costly divorce that I felt he hadn't deserved.

Allison was a gentle man, and Ikey, clever and wonderful in her way, was anything but gentle. Nonetheless, while she was dying, he'd turn up at her bedside in the hospice, and a couple of times I found him there massaging her feet. Months after she died, I met him in Berkeley for breakfast. I explained how impressed I was that he became so supportive of Ikey before her death, despite their nine-year divorce.

'Ikey was a warrior,' he laughed. 'That woman loved a fight. I figured that she must have come into the world that way.'

I had never applied that word to her, but of course he was right. All my life I'd seen my mother at battle, whether it was with me, who resisted her firm control, or the Philadelphia Board of Education in the '50s, who tried to resist her demand to get her three kids into a school in all-white Chestnut Hills in Richmond. Then there was her battle in '64 to buy a home in all-white Kensington, California. Whenever my mother laid down her gauntlet, she was ready to fight to the death. She'd inherited her fighting instincts from her mother, Edna, who was part of our household. Edna was a hell-raiser, and when she and Ikey locked horns, the best thing to do was stand back. In my Dublin hospital bed that Wednesday before dawn, while I lay musing about the Amazons, I chuckled about my mother and her mother, two generations of female warriors.

Thankfully, of the various things I needed to fight, pain wasn't one. My anaesthetist had done a brilliant job. I hadn't had pain on waking from surgery, and that Wednesday morning, I still wasn't feeling any. I hadn't yet used the wrist apparatus that I had been given for what's called 'pain management'. It was an intravenous drip fed into a small contraption on my wrist, which allowed me to administer small doses of morphine when necessary. It seemed something of a miracle that I'd been cut up and sewn up and had tubes coming from me, yet nothing hurt.

Apart from pain, another thing I wasn't going to have to fight was self-pity, since I didn't think it was particularly tragic to lose my breast. Although the eleven days following prognosis had passed quickly, especially with the trip to France and two days of filming, the scheduled surgery and the knowledge that a cancerous tumour had to be eliminated had hung over my head. Now it was gone. History. And with it the breast, but it was needed for nothing in particular. Twelve days earlier I'd said as much to Arnie Hill during my second visit. Now that he'd done the job, my attitude about having a mastectomy remained unchanged. Losing a breast was no big deal, and I wasn't going to make it one. Nor did I regret not having reconstructive surgery at the time of my operation.

I was glad that I'd had the good sense to realise that my surgery and healing was going to be complex enough without further complicating the process by having Arnie try to create a new breast from muscles and flesh that were perfectly in tact. Needing the lymph gland removed under my right arm was complication enough and the full repercussions of that had yet to register.

What I was going to have to fight was being waited on hand and foot during my ten-day hospital stay. It was important to resist too much help, since I was going to have none at the chalet.

I was alone and very conscious of the fact. I was also very aware that things can go wrong after surgery, so I needed to stay strong, remember to speak up for myself at all times, and mind my back in the way that I'd minded Alan's in '99. To be ready for problems, but at the same time not to anticipate any is a skill I learned as a single parent and one I took for granted. It had been useful when Alan got cancer and now that I was on my back, I thought it was going to be useful again.

When I heard stirring in the hospital corridor, as the night nurses started to make their early-morning rounds, I figured it was nearly time to put my war paint on. Something I learned as a cancer carer is that looking good makes people think that you feel good, and if they think that you feel good, they're less likely to inflict their 'poor you' sympathy.

The young Irish nurse who set me up with a basin of water, my toothbrush and wash cloth didn't know how badly I needed to brush my teeth. It felt as though a small furry animal had died in my mouth, and it was amazing how the combination of brushing my teeth and feeling warm water on my face gave me a sense of renewal. I almost felt like me and nearly looked like me in my magnified hand mirror. My hair was in the two buns, one above each ear, that I was wearing when I collected Karis and Mazie from the airport in August. So I took the pins out and loosened the buns, running my fingers through my hair.

Then it was time for the war paint. Lipstick. Blusher. Mascara. Eyeliner. Powder. All of these were in my make-up bag in the tall bedside table, which was sensibly designed for invalids. Like a Lazy Susan, it turned so that all the compartments could be reached without too much stretching. I slipped on the diamond earrings that Mick had got me.

Not until I tried to apply the mascara did I know that my hand was shaky. I felt a little woozy sitting up but didn't know how weak I was until I'd completed these morning ablutions. After that small effort, I was slightly dizzy, but it was worth it because when the nurse came to take my temperature, the first thing she did was smile. 'Don't you look well,' she said.

'I feel it,' I lied. Or maybe it wasn't a lie. I had a sense of completion. Something that had to be done had been achieved. Tumour gone and I was alive.

*I wish I could show you . . . the
astonishing light of your being.*

HAFEZ

11

Friends

Before my mastectomy, had anybody asked, 'What do you fear about what's about to happen?' I would have said, 'Nothing.' Yet I was so relieved, no, so *ecstatic*, not to be in any pain that it suggests to me that subconsciously I was expecting some. To have none made me bold and frisky, because having mentally prepared myself for pain and the combination of patience and energy required to heal, when there was no pain, the work was reduced by a third.

That nothing hurt was a great blessing, which isn't to say that the two plastic tubes inserted in my right side to drain my wound caused no discomfort, or that being incapable of raising my right arm didn't bother me. The restricted use of my right arm continually reminded me that my body had been cut, deeply wounded, traumatised.

When using the toilet only a few feet from my bed or taking a little exercise along the corridor, I had to pick up and hold both plastic bottles collecting the fluid draining from my wound and also manoeuvre the tall metal stand on wheels which held the drip feeding a saline solution into my left arm.

Although this was a nuisance, it was painless. Being without pain was something I never forgot to be grateful for. When I said a few words of thanks before meals, or when I prayed, I always remembered to be grateful that I was in no pain.

Forty-eight hours after my operation, the second day into December, I sat propped up in bed chomping the three-course lunch that I'd ordered and assuming that the worst was over. So much had taken place after my month in Manhattan that I jotted a short list of what had been accomplished in 18 days. Finding the right breast doctor had been the most important, because that led to the quick discovery that I had cancer. Alerting family and friends and having the mastectomy scheduled in ten days was as lucky as finding the chalet and allowing my experience to become a documentary. Everything had happened so fast that it seemed miraculous that I'd gone from discovery to the healing process in less than three weeks.

It was Thursday. Eamon and a cameraman and a sound guy filmed that morning. Now, with the squadron of nurses outside my door, I could relax for a minute. Gazing at the sky and golf course outside my window, I was calm and able to appreciate being there and being alive. Nibbling the comfort of ice cream and jelly, I felt safe and protected in that narrow hospital bed. Rather than feeling silly that I'd risked my life for my Jimi book, I felt that I'd accomplished something, even though I realised that I was only past the first stage of what everyone predicted would be a tough ride.

Thus far, despite my cancer having metastasised from my breast into three lymph nodes, it had been brought under control. Or had it? The disease has such an unpredictable progression that there was no pretending that I was cured before I received the detailed medical breakdown of my amputated breast and malignant tumour.

I'd always thought of cancer as being a bit of decay on the body, a bit like mould on a tomato. If you spot the mould when it's in one small, isolated area, it's easy to remove, but there's no saving a tomato that's riddled with mould. I hoped that in a week, having removed all the body rot that the CAT scan found, I'd be able to reclaim my independence, once again be in full control, be able to cook, clean, drive and write.

But the value of being hospitalised was that I was about to discover how rich in friends I am. It was like waking to find I owned diamond mines. It was even a bit embarrassing.

Whether it was an e-mail on my BlackBerry or a get well card, a friend ringing or making the time to visit, whether it was flowers arriving or a gift in the post, the attention I got overwhelmed me. And I doubt that any of my visitors knew that the energy they left behind in my room was as distinctive and lingering as the perfume of the tall white lilies that came from Charlie Watts and his wife, Shirley.

My visitors ranged in age from eleven to eighty-five, with Stefan Davies of Bally Bla, near the Bel Air, being the youngest. We first met when he was four and I was fifty, and though I can well remember our first outing one rainy afternoon, I can't recall where or how we met. But from the outset, with his old-school manners of please and thank you, his thick mop of brown hair and those wide, inquisitive eyes, Stefan seemed destined to be a beauty and a charmer, like his mother, Christine. Nothing could better describe him than a poem he wrote aged ten, which I had taped to the bedside stand in my hospital room.

> I would like to eat the gentle murmur of a computer
> and the loneliness of a star
> I would like to create an Island off the coast of Ireland

built out of the smell of flowers
I wish I could measure an echo in a cave
I would like to save everything ever said to me and
    keep it in a bottle
I would hate to taste the feel of greed
I would love to melt sadness

When Christine brought Stefan from his boarding school for a hospital visit, they came bearing gifts. As pretty as the red tie-dyed shawl was, it didn't hold a candle to his poem about the goldfish I'd got him when he was four. It had long since died and I'd got two replacements, which he'd named Breakfast and Lunch. He viewed the world with such clarity and wit that, despite his youth, he seemed old and wise, and I always felt that I'd been in the presence of someone special whenever I saw him.

The same could have been said of 18-year-old Max McGuinness, who arrived at the hospital with two beautiful black-and-white photos that he'd taken when he'd visited me in France. One was of the white horse that lives in the meadow next door. The other, which Max had taken at my request, was of a tomb in the village cemetery with la montagne, my writing studio, looking like a white speck upon the hill in the far distance.

'Oh shit, Max,' I said when he handed me the two 8 x 10s, 'a picture of that old tomb in the village graveyard and the one of a pale horse might not be such a great thing to hang in this room. Do you think that it might be too pointed with me here maybe dying of cancer?'

We enjoyed a good laugh about it, but when he left, I taped it to the bathroom mirror. Max's passion for taking pictures had been so much part of him the summer of 2003 when he'd come to hang out with me at my French writing studio. As unusual as our friendship was, as with my relationship with Stefan, it was vital to me. The two of them were such unique boys, if only for the fact that they spent time with a woman aged 58.

The possibility of dying intensified my appreciation of everyone I valued, and in that hospital room, my friends were like good books that one picks up and in reading again, discovers something new. For instance, I discovered that when he crossed the sill of my hospital room, Max had an air of appeasement that he otherwise lacked. I know no one who is so good at turning my simplest statement into a debate. And Stefan's questions about how I was feeling made me ache for the degree of sensitivity in a boy of 11.

The hospital's visiting hours are from 11 a.m. to 9 p.m., and considering how much of a hermit I'd become working on my Jimi book, I suddenly felt like a party girl with people coming and going.

When my very busy English friend, the film and television producer Tony Garnett, whom I'd known since '68, flew in from London with wonderful books and treated me to a couple of hours of his company before turning around to fly back, his making time for that visit wasn't lost on me. Although a sitcom he produced called *Ballykiss Angel* had once made the London to Dublin flight path as familiar to him as to a homing pigeon, he was now working on another series and a day's work had been lost.

Irish friends would drop by after a long working day and pretend not to be tired. Their time, with stories of the world beyond my hospital room, made me feel connected.

Mary Elizabeth Mastrantonio wrote words to the effect that she would have loved to have come had she not been on stage nightly at the Donmar Warehouse in London. Delivering her note and the beautiful toiletries that she'd wrapped was her husband, Pat O'Connor, who strolled into my hospital room as coolly as if he'd dropped in from across town.

'Christ, Pat, I must be dying for you to come all the way from London.' That he's a close friend of my son-in-law's adds to my sense of Pat being family.

'Was that *the* Pat O'Connor?' a nurse asked when he left, because Pat's one of Ireland's best-loved film directors.

'Yes,' I said. But to me it's the sort of husband and father he is that makes him a great man. Just as another visitor, Peter Doyle, I consider a giant among men because of the way he herds his brother John's sheep. The meningitis Pete got as a toddler left him mentally and physically impaired, but he's good at some chores, like feeding the chickens each morning and herding John's flock back and forth to pasture. We became friends when I was using my friend Dana Wynter's cottage in Glenmacnass as a writing hideaway. The Doyle clan are her neighbours in the glen, and one Saturday, when I was reclaiming her garden, I employed Pete as my assistant to cart away branches as I cut them down. His most endearing feature is that when he talks to himself, he admits all the things he's too well-brought up to say aloud. 'She's a silly fool. Look at what she's doing,' he might say as an aside, but he also had the willingness to see my best efforts as good enough, which was something I needed to learn.

'How d'you think I'm doing?' I had asked that Saturday as he watched me up on Dana's stone walls sawing chunky branches. But my sawing leaves a lot to be desired.

'Fine, Marcie. Couldn't be better,' he'd call as I'd snap off a poorly sawn branch and drop it down to him. Then he'd complain aloud about me to himself.

After lunch on 6 June 2004 at Mick's French chateau, with Mick, Keith Richards and Pierre, their sound engineer. (© MARSHA HUNT)

With Mick's chef after lunch at the chateau. (© MARSHA HUNT)

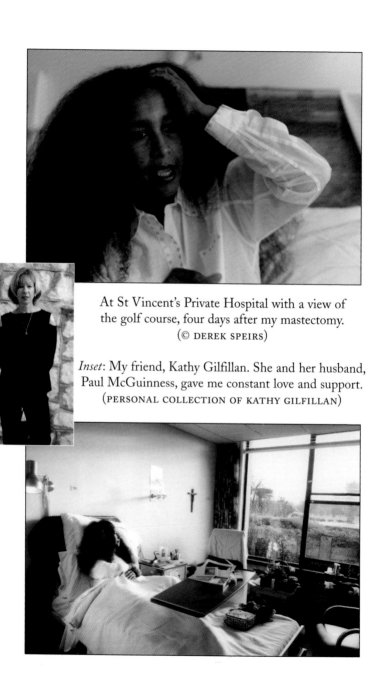

At St Vincent's Private Hospital with a view of the golf course, four days after my mastectomy.
(© DEREK SPEIRS)

Inset: My friend, Kathy Gilfillan. She and her husband, Paul McGuinness, gave me constant love and support.
(PERSONAL COLLECTION OF KATHY GILFILLAN)

Max brought pictures of la montagne and I pasted
Stephan's poem to my bedside table.
(© DEREK SPEIRS)

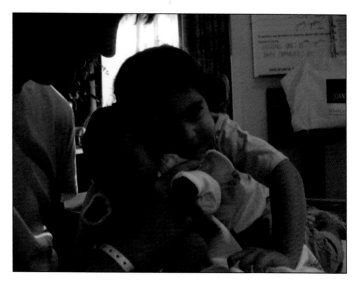

Mazie with her new brother, Zachary, and Jonathan
at Cedars Sinai in LA. (© KARIS JAGGER)

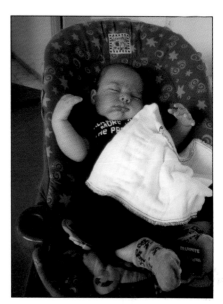

Zachary, six weeks old
and asleep at the hair-
cutting party.
(© FABIENNE TOBACK)

At the hair-cutting party. Left to right: Charis, Sheila, Enid, Andrea and Karis braid my hair.
(© FABIENNE TOBACK)

Mazie cutting Grammy's hair.
(© FABIENNE TOBACK)

Hassan Shuman shaving my head at the hair-cutting party.
(© FABIENNE TOBACK)

Jade, her daughter, Amba, Mick, Mazie, and Karis holding Zach. (© MARSHA HUNT)

Jade's daughter, Sisi, Mick, Karis and Dan, with his back to the camera, being introduced to baby Violet Leitch, who's in the arms of her father, Donovan, the son of Enid Graddis and the folk singer Donovan. (© MARSHA HUNT)

Me with Noel Redding and his girlfriend
Deborah McNaughton at their home,
Dunowen, in Ardfield, which he bequeathed to
her when he died. He was the original bass
player with the Jimi Hendrix Experience.
(© MARSHA HUNT)

Inset: Deborah McNaughton, 1953–2005.
(© JUNE HOUSDEN)

La montagne, my French writing retreat. (© MARSHA HUNT)

At the Mater Private Hospital
with pneumonia.
(© DEREK SPIERS)

Inset: April 10, in hospital with
pneumonia.
(© DEREK SPIERS)

Sweating while I raked dead pine branches, I asked, 'Think it looks OK, Pete?'

'Couldn't be better, Marcie, couldn't be better,' which was the same thing he said as I butchered Dana's hedges. Pete's positivity renewed my own. After I left the glen, I would never visit without dropping in on him, and often when I was abroad, I'd send him a postcard. For the Irish, when a friend is sick, visiting hospital seems to be about personal honour as well as duty, so I rang his brother, John, to ask if he'd bring Pete to the hospital, although the journey was over an hour each way. But all the Doyles knew that Pete and I were friends and that every card or picture that I sent made it to a section on Pete's kitchen wall reserved for me.

He's an important friend, and to see him sitting in my hospital room, head bowed, while he whispered to himself, clutching a big box of chocolates, was healing for me, and I knew that he'd enjoy telling his neighbours in the glen, like Clodagh Duff, that he'd been to see me.

'Clodagh was here yesterday,' I told him to get him talking, while his brother, John, sat by respectfully. 'Seen Clodagh lately, Pete?'

'Came by Sat'day,' he said, having a chuckle and whispering something to himself.

Clodagh's rustic house amongst the trees beside the Doyles' was on 40 acres that John hired to graze his sheep. It was her place that I'd gone to from Room 8 at the Bel Air after my night of phoning friends and family to say that I had cancer. Now Clodagh was stopping by to visit me so often, I told Pete. 'And do you like this shawl I got from her and Ib?' I asked, pointing to the pale-green pashmina that I'd hung over the head of my bed.

Ib Jorgensen, who has a Dublin art gallery, is Clodagh's

partner. The champagne they'd brought me was in the small fridge with the champagne and chocolates from Ted and Marie Doyle. 'Cancer's been good to me,' I assured Pete's brother, John, as they were leaving. But that didn't belie the fact that it's also lethal. My friend Deborah McNaughton, suffering with breast cancer in Santa Fe, had yet to say in her e-mails that her disease was spreading to other vital organs.

It was early days for me. I assumed that some of my visitors left the hospital certain that I had one foot in the grave, because the mystery of cancer, the absence of a sure cure, keeps everyone guessing about who'll die once afflicted. Doesn't everyone have a theory about why people survive?

'Oh, you'll live,' I heard so often, to which I replied, 'Maybe not.'

But the truth is that I felt strong, until I had so many visitors that it was zapping my energy. I recalled how when Alan was ill, it sometimes got to the point that I asked friends not to come, because visitors can take more energy than they give. There were more than a few times that I sat in that hospital bed listening to the woes of people who believed that they had come to make me feel better.

'Listen,' I'd say, 'try singing. It's good for getting rid of the blues. Good for the lungs, good for the soul and great for expelling pent-up energy.'

I believe it. But it was hard to have a good sing in that bed, so as soon as I was strong enough, I'd slip down late at night to the empty chapel and sing. Out of respect for it being a religious space, I restricted my songs to spirituals, but I know so few that more than once I resorted to 'Nobody Knows the Trouble I've Seen'. One round of 'Wade in the Water' would have me on the verge of giggling, because I'd think about Edna, my mother's mother, singing it when she was madder than hell over something like being left to wash dishes after having fried chicken for the family on Sunday.

'Singing heals,' I've been saying for years. As do the prayers and positive energy of friends. After three days in hospital, when the drip was removed from my arm, I slipped my feet into Karis's slippers to walk visitors to the elevator.

'Come on,' said one, as I marched along beside him holding the two bags which contained the plastic bottles into which the tubes in my side were draining. 'You're an actress. Do you really feel OK, or are you just acting it?'

'I keep telling people that cancer's been good for me.'

But I'd soon stop singing that tune.

Any idiot can face a crisis. It's the day to day living that wears you out.

ANTON CHEKHOV

12

11 December 2004

Make-up on, hair down, and I'm standing in my robe and pyjamas in front of St Vincent Private's elaborate Nativity scene. It was so big that it took up a large portion of the entrance. 'Where's baby Jesus?' I asked the grey-haired hospital porter, who was manning the reception desk alone.

'He doesn't come till the 25th,' he said. I should have known.

The straw in the manger was real, but considering that Mary was about to drop a baby, she didn't look a bit pregnant, and as I took a seat nearby in the small, deserted reception, I was trying to remember when I'd ever seen her portrayed as very pregnant.

It was so dark beyond the glass wall overlooking the parking lot that it could have been night. Instead, it was morning, Seven thirty and the fairy lights on the maroon Christmas decorations were still on. I loved sitting there while the staff straggled in, dressed in their own clothes as opposed to hospital uniforms. Whether it was a tea lady, a nurse, or one of the clerical staff, in their street clothes, they seemed to carry a less detached air. Their personal dress sense also told a lot more about them than the crisp hospital uniforms.

As each entered, they brought in the cold. Walking ice cubes they were, passing me in my robe and pyjamas. I was so relieved that I had a good excuse for not stepping out into that icy dawn.

Sitting there broke the morning monotony, but otherwise that Saturday, 11 December 2004, had begun like every other hospital day. And at that stage, even before hell broke loose, I recognised that getting too cosy with the hospital's routine was dangerous. I wasn't an employee. The place wasn't my life. I was passing through, and it was no good allowing myself to settle in.

Having been there two days longer than expected, my stuff was packed. Kathy had taken all my books home and sent Kevin to collect a suitcase. All my instincts were telling me it was time to go. Get out. Move on. I wonder now, had I listened, would things have played out differently? On the other hand, it's possible that I was already in trouble that Saturday morning and just didn't read the signs.

Rain or shine, and there's not much shine in Dublin in December, after rising at six thirty to tidy my room and freshen my glut of flowers from friends, someone from the catering staff would arrive a half an hour or so later to give me a fresh pitcher of drinking water, and our daily dialogue hardly changed. When she'd enter the room and head for the window, carrying a clean tray with the clean glass and pitcher, I'd say, 'Morning, how are you?' She'd say, 'Fine, and you?' to which I'd say, 'Fine, thanks.' She'd leave the tray on the sill, and no sooner than she was out the door, I'd move it to the table, beside the orchids from Keith.

Then, while the two night nurses would be busy getting

patients on the ward ready for a new day, I'd close my door and begin my morning ablutions in the still silence of my clinically white bathroom. Sometimes I could hear the TV in the room above mine or a trolley moving up or down the corridor outside, but there were never voices or footsteps, and the fact that it would remain dark out for quite some time gave a false feeling that the world was sleeping when, in fact, the streets of Dublin were crawling with morning traffic: people rushing to get to work, kids rushing to get to school. But my room overlooking the golf course offered no sign of that.

Being a good patient is tiring. I tried to be so independent and helpful that anybody would have thought that I was collecting brownie points. A couple of times I even helped a nurse to change my bed, because she came alone. Normally they worked in twos. However it may have appeared to anyone else, I was doing myself the favour, because it meant that when I returned home to do everything alone, it would seem less difficult.

Occasionally, I'd let myself rest, but for someone like me who works in isolation and silence, being a prisoner in that bed was work, because, night and day, people needing TLC entered my room uninvited. Take the cleaning staff, who were all foreign, mostly from eastern Europe. Pretending that they weren't there was unacceptable, and when I enquired about their lives before Dublin, I learned that they'd all been professionals of some sort. To discover that the man cleaning my toilet was a lawyer from Croatia was no more shocking than discovering that the Russian mother who dusted was a teacher, or that the tall Chinese fellow wielding the vacuum was a businessman in China.

It takes energy to coddle strangers, as the medical staff would have agreed, and they too needed stroking. The nurses on the ward were friendly, but scratch beneath the surface and they each had stories. There were a couple of odd ones who were so miserable that I sensed it enter my room with them. It was work to make them feel appreciated. I find it impossible to be oblivious to other people's energy, and some strike me as an open book, they're so easy to read. Perhaps that's why I couldn't read a book there.

But it would be wrong to suggest that it was all work, because there were loads of the staff that I looked forward to seeing, from the porters at reception whom I visited at night, to nurses like Orla and Edward, who injected such warmth and caring into the job that one wondered how they had any left for their families when they got home. Knowing that Arnie would visit me smiling, when he had so many other patients to attend to, made me think about the four small boys whose images I had seen on his mobile phone.

I looked forward to my anaesthetist, Dr Alan McShane, dropping by to say hello, and I was forever begging him to tell me what potion he'd given me prior to surgery that eliminated my pain. Whether he popped by to say hello in a suit or his surgical greens, a chat with him for a minute or two was as good as any friend's visit.

The only intrusion I hated was having my temperature taken. Without warning, a nurse would arrive with a tall trolley of computerised apparatus, part of which gets poked in your ear. Along with it is the blood pressure machine.

Mornings were busy, with the catering staff arriving with food and water, the newspaper vendor, a nurse to check my blood pressure and temperature, another to change the two plastic bottles collecting fluid from my wound. Considering the solitary writing life that I was used to, I'd been ticking off the days till Friday, 10 December, when I had expected to be getting back to my solitude.

On Saturday morning, 11 December, however, I was still there. A situation I had neither anticipated nor desired. Apart from anything else, there was a virus, one of those hospital superbugs, attacking patients, staff and visitors at St Vincent's Private, as well as the big public teaching hospital to which it's attached. While I was down in reception, there was a big sign posted beside the Nativity scene, which said that, due to the winter vomiting bug, visiting was restricted and children were not allowed. And two days earlier, poor Kathy, thinking that it was safe to run in and collect a bag of my books, had caught the bug.

Of the many friends I warned to stay away, one was Mary Banotti, who ran for the Irish presidency back in 1997. We met when I became the writer-in-residence at Mountjoy Prison in Dublin. She was helping an African nurse who was incarcerated in the female prison.

Most of the prisoners taking my writing workshops were heroin addicts, and, collectively, their true stories produced such a telling picture of addiction, I asked Mainstream to publish them as *The Junkyard: Voices of an Irish Prison*. Mary was one of the politicians who was most supportive when promoting the book prompted me to begin setting up a research and rehabilitation study centre. But it was a huge project, and, as my baby, demanded my undivided attention. Unfortunately, when Alan got cancer, I was forced to drop it.

Mary and I remained in touch, however, and on that Saturday morning she rang to say that her houseguest, Anne Jocelyn, who'd been involved with Noel Redding when he played bass in the Jimi Hendrix Experience, was eager to meet me. I was excited. I'd been 12 days in hospital and was raring to get back to finish my Jimi book.

Since Mary lives not far from the hospital, I said, 'How

about I hop in a cab and come to you? I'm being allowed out for little jaunts this weekend.'

It was true. The previous night when Arnie Hill came to check on me, he was surprised to find me lying with my feet at the head of the bed and my head at the foot.

'*Anything* for a change,' I said, trying to smile but sounding fed up.

'That bored, are you?'

'If only you knew! I'm desperate. I was scheduled to be discharged, but Claire said today that it was best to stay.'

Claire Grenane, the breast-care nurse, had advised me to remain in the hospital over the weekend, so that I'd be an in-patient when the hospital's oncologist, Professor John Crown, returned from a big breast cancer convention in Texas. She said that as an in-patient, I'd have a better chance of being scheduled for chemotherapy, which was to be the next stage of my treatment. I took some convincing, because Baby John Ladner, with whom I'd been friends since we were Berkeley freshmen, was due from LA on Monday to spend a night at my Bel Air chalet.

It's no wonder that my instincts were telling me to check out of the hospital: not only was I scared of the winter vomiting bug, but also, for the first time, I'd been in excruciating pain, when the loose flap of skin made by the incision to hold the tube draining my wound was taped down in the wrong direction. It was accidental, so I didn't complain, but I thought, 'Time to get outta here.'

So on Friday night, 10 December, as I lay sprawled upside down on the bed, I could have kissed Arnie Hill, when he said, 'I think you're up to taking a few outings. Treat the place like a hotel. The St Vincent's Hotel.'

That gave me the opportunity to accept Mary Banotti's

invitation to pop over and meet her friend, Anne Jocelyn. 'I'm already dressed,' I told Mary. 'I'll order a taxi and see you in half an hour.'

It seemed good fortune and a good omen that, despite being in hospital, I was getting an unexpected interview for the book. I was doubly eager to meet Anne, because her affair with Noel Redding had taken place within weeks of his marriage, which he'd always insisted ended before the ink had dried on the marriage licence.

His refusal to acknowledge the son born to his estranged Swedish wife, who had returned to Sweden, led to the son contesting Noel's will after Noel's unexpected death on 11 May 2002. Noel had left his house to his American girlfriend, Deborah McNaughton, with whom he was living when I first interviewed him there in West Cork in January 2000. After Noel's death, my sympathy and affection for him transferred to Deborah, since I knew how devoted he'd been to her. I was not only sorry that his will had submerged her in a legal battle but I also often reminded her that, after two years, her continued struggle to hold on to the house was interfering with her cancer recovery.

Now, on 11 December 2004, two weeks away from what would have been Noel's 60th birthday, Deborah's legal fight was forging ahead and so was her cancer. It had metastasised to other organs, so she'd moved from the house in West Cork to return to her sister's in Santa Fe, and I was hoping that Anne Jocelyn might be able to shed light on Deborah's inheritance problem.

As the taxi ferried me from the hospital to Mary's at 9 a.m. that Saturday morning, I was surprised that after 12 days in the hospital, the world outside it looked alien. I was feeling the cold as the car rolled along, and I was also homesick for my freedom. Cancer had robbed me of my hard-won independence.

Luckily, Anne Jocelyn didn't think it odd that I finally had to shift from a chair to the floor to interview her during my hour at Mary's. I knew that I was too weak to sit up unless I sat cross-legged, Navajo style. The interview went OK, but boy was I grateful for the lift back to the hospital. Slipping back along the ward corridor more quietly than usual, I was glad to see my bed, unaware that my exhaustion may have been an early sign that I had picked up a hospital superbug.

It was late afternoon and the sun was setting before I felt up to going out again, this time to visit an 85-year-old friend, Nora Doyle, whose fall had landed her in a nursing home near the hospital. Since the same nursing home was recommended as a place that I could go for residential care if I felt too weak to cope at home alone, it would also be a good opportunity to check it out.

'Oh fuck, not this,' I murmured, no sooner than I crossed the doorsill.

Despite being 58, in my head I was still a wild thing of 13, who loved to dance, shout and run about, and saw breast cancer as another mad adventure. But could it reduce me to even a few days among these elderly residents with their zimmer frames and hearing aids? The thought scared me out of my wits, and after sitting five minutes in the dining room with Nora, I was ready to run screaming out of there. I scurried to the parking lot, where my friend, Eithne Mulherne, who had given me a lift, was keeping her car warm for me.

'You OK? What happened?' she asked.

'Please God that I never have to wind up there . . .'

But what cancer had taught me is that you never know what will happen next.

Later that evening, I was glad to be between the starched white sheets of my hospital bed when the bedside phone rang at seven thirty. Propped up on a mound of pillows, I grabbed it.

'Hello?'

'Hey,' said Jonathan.

Hearing my son-in-law's voice, made my heart stop. 'Karis?'

'She did fine.'

'Shit! Oh shit, JW! You mean she had that baby?'

'He weighs seven pounds, fifteen ounces. She did great.'

'Wooooo Hoooo!' I hollered, and sat up in bed. 'Dammit! I knew that baby was comin' early just like Mazie. When d'you get back?

'Just in time.'

He'd been shooting on location in Berlin, and explained that having insisted that he leave a few days early to return to LA, he'd managed to get back hours before Karis went into labour.

'Ricky delivered him?'

'Yeah.'

I could just imagine their nativity scene in a fancy, high-tech delivery room at Cedars Sinai, with Ricky Hendrix, Karis's African-American obstetrician, in command. Having watched him deliver Mazie on 25 July 2001 while Mick and I stood watch, I knew that Karis was in good, strong Hendrix hands.

Jonathan sounded tired. 'Are you wrecked, JW?' I asked, grinning as I pulled the heavy yellow cotton blanket up to my chin, because I was feeling cold. 'Straight from that shoot, on a transatlantic flight, to stand by Karis in labour was no easy call. You mind yourself.'

'I'm fine. How're you is more to the point?'

'Shit. I've got a grandson, so now you know I'm good.'

*You got to know when
to leave the party.*

DORIS TROY

13

Hard-Headed

Having spent the night knowing that Karis was in Cedars Sinai with a new baby boy, I woke on the morning of the 12th as elated as a five year old finding a brand-new doll under the Christmas tree. A baby! A boy! Little league baseball! Fire trucks! Marbles! Bugs! While my mind went into overload with stuff related to little boys, I was also considering the strange coincidence of a daughter being in hospital to do that most glorious female thing, give birth, as opposed to her mother being in hospital to deal with that female dread, breast cancer.

The timing of Karis's labour and her breast feeding a new life in the world got me thinking about nursing mothers and mothers nursing and reaffirmed my sense of the breasts' essential function in Nature's great scheme. It reinforced my belief that losing one of mine, which had outlived its nursing purpose, was of no great loss. Yet our culture has made allure the breasts' primary role. We've exaggerated this to such a degree that women will risk their health getting surgery and implants to improve the appearance of their breasts. And those improvements – to make breasts look bigger and younger – engage the skills of some of our finest surgeons. After gruelling years of education to learn medical feats, they devote their time and talent to doing breast implants.

Cancer couldn't rob me of my breasts' essential purpose. Age had done it long ago. And that loss was a natural part of my ageing process, which, like saggy breasts, is another thing that we women are encouraged to hold in contempt and fear. Not that I did.

I woke that Sunday with no wish to turn back the clock, no wish to be a nursing mother. I loved becoming a grandmother for the second time and was raring to celebrate. There'd been no boys born in my family since my brother in 1943, which was another reason to mark the arrival of my grandson, Zachary Millard Watson. What I really wanted to do was get on a plane and be of service to my daughter, as I'd done when Mazie was born. But this time all I could do was have a mastectomy.

'What to wear and where to go?' I was asking myself as I marched along the windowless corridor to the tiny utility room where the clean vases were kept. Having had one of the tubes in my side removed a couple of days earlier, I felt liberated having to tote just one plastic bottle instead of two. Outside my door, I'd lined up my vases filled with flowers, and, having cut the stems, I was busy changing the water. It was a new day in our family, and I wanted my flowers to look fresh.

Having decided that I'd have breakfast at the nearby Four Seasons Hotel followed by a visit to St Patrick's Cathedral to light some candles, being physically capable of tidying my room had me more excited than putting on my make-up and street clothes. Despite feeling weak the day before at Mary Banotti's, my two small jaunts outside the hospital had restored my sense of independence.

Hard-Headed

The real drag about having cancer was the way I was expected to relinquish my power and knowledge of myself. Suddenly, outsiders on the medical staff were supposed to know more about me than I did. Letting others tell me what I had to do and what was best may have seemed like letting the medical staff do their job, but having toted my mind and body around for 58 years, I can intuit things about it and know myself well. Living alone contributed to this, as had my various professions. Having worked over the years at singing and dancing, acting and writing, these disciplines kept me in touch with myself, whether it was breathing properly to sing, being attuned with my body to dance, or being conscious of my emotions in order to act them out or write about them. And apart from my work contributing to my self-awareness, I'd cared for my body, exercised it regularly and eaten clean, wholesome food. As a fish-eating vegetarian, I avoided meat and milk products and all drugs, both social and pharmaceutical. Friends look at me doubtfully when I say that I've never touched cocaine, gave up smoking grass in '66 and nicotine in '78.

Inasmuch as I let a tumour get out of hand for the sake of my work, it may sound implausible to say that I liked my body and respected it. OK, so I was never crazy about my rugby player's thighs and had battles with cake to retain my best weight, but more often than not, every morning upon waking, I'd go through my body, starting with my toes and working upwards, to thank God that everything was operating. Maybe it's relevant that I didn't include my breasts, but then, as I'd said enough times after hearing I was about to lose one, 'Well, the truth is, I wasn't using it for anything.'

At the hospital, after bathing, I liked to examine my wound in the bathroom mirror. I was impatient to have the stitches out and see the scar become a neat line running horizontally from the middle of my chest to my underarm. So imagine my alarm just before midnight on 12 December, after my late bath, when I noticed during my mirror inspection that welts were erupting beneath the narrow strips that had been placed lengthwise across my stitched wound. The strips had been applied by a nurse soon after my outing to the Four Seasons Hotel and St Patrick's Cathedral. Although I'd noticed that she'd applied longer, thinner strips than ones previously used, I said nothing.

Removing one thin strip, then another, I was horrified to see what I automatically assumed was an allergic reaction, because the welts were imprints of the strips. Shocked and frightened, I threw on my robe and went rushing down the deserted corridor to the brightly lit nurses' station to show the two night nurses.

In the spacious visitors' room, where I found both nurses, the lights were as low as the TV's volume. Though one was busy doing paperwork, the other was resting beside the vending machine. Since she had her feet up and her glasses off, I was apologetic, because, prior to my bath, I had been sweating so much that they'd been in to change my sheets.

'Sorry to bother you,' I said. The urgency in my voice was intentional. 'But can you come and take a look at my wound? Something's terribly wrong. I may be allergic to the strips.'

Though her advice was that I go to bed and leave the strips alone, I rushed back to my bathroom for another inspection. When removing more strips produced more welts, I gasped. 'What the fuck's happening?' I said aloud, my eyes wild, as I drew closer to the mirror before turning on my heels and heading back to the dimly lit visitors' room.

'You'll really have to look at this,' I told the small, middle-aged nurse who was still resting beside the vending machine. 'And you won't see anything in the dark.' She was slow to rise, and as I said, 'You'll have to get me a doctor,' my heart began beating faster, a sure sign that I was on the verge of losing my temper.

'You should go back to bed,' she said, though she had yet to put on her glasses.

'I'm telling you there's something wrong!'

'There's nothing can be done until the morning. You should go to bed.' Maybe she thought a calm tone of voice would placate me. Instead, the pleading in my voice flipped to rage.

'If I wanted to stay in a fucking hotel, I'd go down the road to the goddamn Four Seasons! This is a hospital and I need a doctor.'

Had she said that there was no doctor on duty at St Vincent's Private and that one would have to be fetched from the adjoining public hospital, I might've been more sympathetic about her reluctance. Instead, she said nothing, and, rather than grab a fist of her hair, I said, 'Are you aware that a documentary is being made about my stint in this hospital?'

Though I agreed to wait in my room for a doctor to come from the public hospital, I was distressed that I'd had to beg for one and distressed that he was coming from a hospital where the highly contagious winter vomiting bug was so virulent that it had been reported in the newspapers. I became more distressed still when he eventually appeared with the nurse at my bedside and suggested that I take an antibiotic. 'This area is inflamed,' he said, indicating the flesh around my wound. Until then, I hadn't noticed. His skin was as brown as mine. He was Indian or Pakistani.

'An antibiotic? But I would need to take a whole course, and, in light of my mastectomy, if I'm to go on a course of antibiotics, surely it's best if my surgeon prescribes it? He'll be here in six hours. You don't think that this could be an allergic reaction to the strips?'

'I've never seen anything like this,' he said, staring at my chest.

It would be the following day when I heard that a previous patient in the next room had the same reaction. That patient turned out to be someone I would get to know.

'Couldn't I be having an allergic reaction?' I repeated like a broken record, while the small, middle-aged nurse said, 'You should listen to the doctor and take an antibiotic.'

Hard-headed. That's what my grandmother used to call me. Call it whatever you like, I was making my assessment based on the fact that my wound had a dozen welts shaped like the strips which had protected it.

I was so wound up after the doctor and nurse left that I decided to walk to calm myself. As I headed down the hall past the visitors' room and saw the two night nurses there, this hospital, which had made me feel safe and protected, now seemed alien.

On the elevator to the ground floor, a very strange and disconcerting sensation was gradually rising up from my waist on my right side. The area felt as though it was both numb yet freezing, like an iceberg emerging on my side, and this was accompanied by pins and needles. On my way back to my room, when I mentioned this to the small, middle-aged nurse who was still in the visitors' room, her response was that I should have taken the antibiotic that the doctor had wanted to prescribe.

At times like these, the only thing that stops me screaming

is that Rudyard Kipling line, 'If you can keep your head when all about you are losing theirs and blaming it on you.'

Having just had major surgery to eliminate that mysterious disease called cancer, the combination of the welts and the strange freezing sensation down my side troubled me. Convinced that I was having an allergic reaction, I had no idea whether it would subside or escalate. Would I get more skin eruptions? Would it provoke internal problems? Would it interfere with my wound healing?

At 8.30 on Monday morning, when Arnie Hill appeared in my room, I wondered why he said that he was prescribing an intravenous antibiotic before he examined me.

'Are you just going by what that doctor said last night?'

I wanted my surgeon to be as freaked as I was that his 12-day-old incision and neat black stitching was now covered in a dozen raised welts, which I assured him would leave scars. Any stranger looking at the long slit across my chest might have said it looked so bad that a few more scars in that area would hardly matter. But can't Amazons have a little vanity?

It would be Tuesday night before I saw Arnie Hill again.

Nurses came. Nurses went. Catering staff came. Catering staff went. There I was on my back in a Dublin hospital bed with this strange sensation spreading from under my right arm to my waist. Certain that I was having an allergic reaction to the strips which had caused the welts, the hard cold fact that I had to face was that no one believed that I knew my body better than anyone else.

Hard-headed is what my grandmother used to call me. Call it what you like, but throughout that Monday, as I bandied the word allergy about whenever anyone entered my room, I was slowly coming to realise that I faced a cultural problem:

allergies are such an American concept that the hospital had no allergist.

I managed to keep my promise to collect an LA friend at Dublin airport that Monday around 5 p.m. But when my good friend and homoeopath, Marie Doyle, dropped me off at arrivals, she noticed that I couldn't stand up straight. She had taken such pride in how I'd recovered from my mastectomy that I wouldn't say how ill I was feeling or that I'd first noticed feeling weak on Saturday morning when I popped into Mary Banotti's.

By Tuesday afternoon, the reason I now acknowledged being sick was that I couldn't get out of bed. My sole comfort was the view from my window as I watched flocks of black birds fly.

Marie Doyle happened to drop in to see me when Professor Crown, the oncologist back from Texas, was seated in a chair at my bedside trying to tell me of the plans that he had for my chemotherapy. At that stage I was raging with fear, with fever, with anger. Why did no one accept that I was having an allergic reaction to those strips? The street fighter surged in me, and I cursed them both, Marie and the professor, for all I was worth.

'Allergy?' the nurse said, as she rolled in the trolley to take my blood pressure and temperature.

'I think I might be having an allergic reaction,' I'd tell anybody who'd listen.

'Allergy? Allegy!! Allergy . . . allergy . . . Allergy . . . ALLERGY!' How often did I say it and how frustrating was it to discover that my knowledge of my body was irrelevant. I felt like a painting done in '88 by my friend and ex-manager, David Ruffell. He was dying of Aids, and it was those early days when Aids victims were treated like pariahs. His painting of a ghostly figure screaming just about conjures up how I was feeling.

I was sick. My wound was now scarred and inflamed. The notion that I was having an allergic reaction to the strips continued to grip me, and since no one would listen to me, I rang the only person I knew who was well connected in Ireland yet not part of it.

'Mick? Hey, it's Marsha.' He'd last heard my voice two days earlier on Sunday, when I had been gleeful about our newborn grandson. This time he heard me crying. 'Can you help? I need to find Dublin's best allergist.'

When Arnie brought a microbiologist, Professor Billy Hall, I still couldn't read the writing on the wall. I knew that St Vincent's Private was alerting visitors to stay away, because the virus known as the winter vomiting bug was contaminating the hospital. But I knew nothing about the deadly infection MRSA, which was becoming the plague of Irish hospitals. Nor did I have an inkling that I had contracted it.

Baby John Ladner was 58. Six weeks younger than me. When we were 18-year-old freshmen at Berkeley in 1964, I nicknamed him Baby John and have called him that ever since. He was one of the prettiest boys on campus and looked equally good as a middle-age judge presiding over Los Angeles courtrooms. But when I met him at Dublin airport, he wore a leather jacket and jeans, and he was wearing the same thing when he dropped by my hospital room late that Tuesday.

I agreed that my Bel Air chalet would be no fun without me, but when making our plans for him to spend a night at my place before driving on towards Limerick to visit his friend, Gail Getty, an ex-wife of John Paul, we hadn't figured on me still being in hospital and agreed that after a night in a Dublin hotel near the hospital, he would drive to the Gettys'. But the following day, he visited me before setting off.

With Baby John holidaying in Ireland for the first time, I didn't want to tell him how sick I was feeling the day after he'd landed, but he's known me for 40 years and could see that what ailed me was not my mastectomy but something else. After 20 years as a judge, he's a professional listener. He was standing by the window in my hospital room when I said, 'Why will nobody here believe me that I'm having an allergic reaction to those strips? They are plying me with antibiotics and I'm getting the fuck out of here. There's no doctor on duty at night. I'd be better off in that hotel you're staying in.' I was out of my mind with a mixture of fear, rage and a loss of confidence in the care I was getting.

By Wednesday, I couldn't lift my head off the pillow. When my friend, Eithne Mulherne, came to visit, she was shocked by the physical state she found me in. I hadn't combed my hair, because I lacked the strength. When she walked in, it was early evening, dark out and dark in my room. We'd been friends since I worked at Mountjoy Prison, where she'd been secretary to Mountjoy's governor, John Lonergan. Whether Eithne was dealing with prison staff or prisoners, she wasted neither time nor words but was quick to spot someone's need, and she went out and got me food and a bottle of water.

'Eithne, what I really need,' I said after sipping the water, 'is a sample of the strips that were put on my wound when those welts appeared. I think I've got an allergy to them. I feel like I'm fucking dying.'

The nurse on duty did not respond to Eithne's repeated requests for a sample of the strips. Eithne was unmoved. She didn't give up. Three times I watched her slip out of the room but return empty handed. Finally, she managed to get samples of the long narrow strip under which the welts had formed. She also persevered until the nurse on duty gave her a sample of the

152

shorter, wider strip that had previously been used. Now I would be able to have a closer look at them. There are times when people appear in one's life when you can never thank them enough. That Thursday, when Eithne said goodbye, I was feeling about her the way an injured soldier must towards a buddy who's carried him from the battlefield.

When I slipped off early the next morning to the Mater Private Hospital, where I planned to beg for a bed, I knew that the big thing going against me was that Ireland is a village in which everyone is connected. But I was also daring to repeat what I had done for Alan in '99, when I got him out of a ward in St Vincent's Teaching Hospital and into a private room at the Mater Private.

Hard-headed my grandmother used to call me.

Though the sandy-haired woman seated in front of her computer in the Mater Private's small admissions office remembered me from 1999 when Alan was a patient, familiarity counted for nothing in altering the Christmas schedule. Sitting on the floor because I felt too weak to stand, I said, 'You're sure you haven't a private room spare?

She was positive. The weeks either side of Christmas saw the whole of Ireland in holiday spirit, and the revels reduced the number of wards operating during holiday time.

When I crept back into a taxi, I told the driver, 'St Vincent's Private on the Herbert Road, but do you mind stopping at Bewley's Hotel first? I should only be a minute.'

In fact, it took a good five minutes to book a room and get a key card. After checking my watch, I told the pleasant young receptionist who'd asked for my credit card, 'I won't be back until this afternoon with my things.'

As I said to a nurse at the nurses' station on my ward, popping back and forth for my IVs of antibiotics seemed safer than being an in-patient. What with the winter vomiting disease . . .

My surgeon didn't quite agree. Now, Arnie Hill took on my cancer when it was an emergency, and that was no small thing, but having lost confidence in my treatment, I couldn't stay for his sake.

'If I can get you a bed in the Blackrock Clinic . . .' he started.

'When?'

'Let me get back to you.'

Arnie had to have me registered there by another surgeon affiliated with the Blackrock, but he promised that he would continue to look after me there and visit each day. I realised that this was a highly unusual arrangement. I also knew that my health insurance didn't cover me at the Blackrock and that I would have to pay an additional 367 euros a day. I didn't have the money, but I had my AIB visa credit card. It had saved my butt more than once and was about to save me again.

Though Arnie asked if I needed an ambulance, I passed, figuring I could take a cab, but, feeling as ill as I did, I was overwhelmed by the amount of packing I had to do. When Anne Counihan, Tim and Mary's daughter, rang to ask if I was all right, I said. 'I'm really good, because I'm leaving here tonight.'

'Leaving?' She was at a Christmas party. Her voice was a little sparkier than usual, as were her spirits, which are always pretty high. 'Oooh' she said, 'Leaving to go where?'

'The Blackrock Clinic.'

'Can I do anything?'

I nearly said no. But I had so much to do that I said, 'I could use a hand with the packing. Anybody would think that I'd been here for months with all the stuff I've accumulated.'

Anne was soon dropped off at the hospital in a taxi. Finding books and papers piled around my room, she said, 'I'll do these!'

'Better that you do my bathroom,' I said, oblivious to the fact that I should've been quarantined and the last thing she should have been doing without rubber gloves was handling anything in my bathroom.

Though I was relieved to close the door to that room with its splendid view, I was also a little sad to slip away with no goodbye. That space was imbued with the sweetest memories of kindnesses from friends and the medical staff, whether it was an extra biscuit from the tea lady, or a quick visit from Lillian, the auxiliary nurse, or that unexpected visit from Clodagh Duff's sister, Maggie, or the young Asian registrar coming to say hello – I'd had such happy times there in that room until things went quickly downhill after 12 December.

Every blade of grass has its angel that bends over and whispers, 'Grow, grow.'

TALMUD

14

White Christmas

Jimi was black rock. Five years of my life I'd devoted to explaining the how and why of that. My life risked for the how and why of that. My breast gone for the how and why of the king of black rock.

For me, who's forever on the lookout for signs and omens, the hospital's name, the Blackrock Clinic, signified that I'd come to the right place. For me, transferring there was about finding safety, because discovering that there was no night duty doctor at St Vincent's Private made me feel unsafe. I didn't care that one could be summoned from the neighbouring hospital, my idea of hospitals is that there are doctors available 24 hours a day.

When I checked in that Friday night at the Blackrock, with Anne Counihan having escorted me there in a taxi, I had to register at the reception desk and was asked for my credit card in the same way that it had been requested at Bewley's Hotel earlier that day. It made registering at the hospital seem like a business transaction. I made little of the fact that I was feeling ill, but as soon as Anne saw I was safe and said goodbye, I was relieved to be placed in the care of a nurse also named Anne before an Asian doctor came to talk to me.

Being alone with no advocate made me extremely aware of the fact that I was at the mercy of the good intentions of the medical staff. The doctor probably thought I was crazy when I held his hand and burst into tears, but the effort and will it had taken to get myself to a safe place when I was so ill made me weep for Me. For days, I'd been saying allergy, and no one had listened. For days, I had felt as though I was being ignored, powerless in a hospital bed, placating the medical staff as they plied me with antibiotics which I thought were useless, and to some extent at the Blackrock Clinic, my instincts were proven right. But how I came to realise this came as a shock that had me reeling.

It began with the fact that I wake for a few hours every night. It's such a normal sleep pattern for me that not only did I refuse the sleeping pills offered, I drew pleasure from being awake when the hospital was, as it were, sleeping. Slipping on my robe and slippers, and pushing a wheelchair for support, I was able to leave my room and go exploring. Though I was looking for nothing in particular, there were always little discoveries to be made, passing the nurses quietly working at their station or the porter in the lobby reading his book. The writer in me liked the sensation of observing while not being observed during a ride in the elevator to the lobby or creeping slowly along the corridor on my floor, past the ever so well-equipped cardiology ward. The still and quiet halls had an element of suspense, and when I slipped back into bed, it was nice to have a clear sense of what lay beyond my room.

It therefore felt as much an affront as a surprise when, after I'd been in the hospital for a few days, one afternoon a nurse, finding me in bed, admonished me for leaving my room. As she stood there saying that I had to remain in my room, I imagined that there were any number of silly official reasons for her instruction, safety hazards and fire hazards among them. But after what had happened the night of 12 December, I wasn't about to let myself get riled by another nurse.

'Excuse me,' I said curtly, 'but I'm a patient in this hospital, not a prisoner.'

'You have MRSA. You must stay in your room.' That she was suggesting that I had a lethal, communicable and hard-to-cure disease caused by poor hygiene among staff in hospitals almost made me laugh. I didn't even know what the letters stood for.

'MRSA? And since when did I have MRSA?'

'You came in with it.' Her accusation had become even more absurd to me.

'Says who?' Indignant, I sat up higher in bed.

'It's on your admission record.' She was serious. I was stunned.

'You're telling me that I came in here with bloody MRSA?'

While she went away to get confirmation, her news had me shaking. I was ready to declare war and would have done so had I not realised that I was in a dicey situation. I was always conscious that in Ireland, everybody was so connected that you never knew exactly who you were talking to. I recently learned that I was one of thousands who had not been informed that they had MRSA. How could I make a stink? Who could I trust?

MRSA is known as a staph infection in the States, and it's a hospital plague that means that, if you are unlucky enough to catch it, you could leave the hospital with more problems than you had when you entered.

Knowing that I had MRSA explained why my wound was

constantly filling up with a pink fluid which I had been expressing down the bathroom sink to avoid having it drained by Arnie Hill with what I called a horse needle. It was connected to a large syringe into which the fluid was siphoned off. The needle was actually a tube and it was so thick and the pain so excruciating when it pierced my flesh that it became a matter of honour to resist screaming when I had to go through the process, which only my surgeon could do. I'd taken to calling Arnie 'Dracula', and would make jokes as soon as I saw that needle coming at me, but it was bravado to deflect the pain.

I've failed to mention that on that same Friday that I booked into Bewley's Hotel and was eventually taken in at the Blackrock Clinic, I'd noticed that of the two types of bandages that had been used, the long thin strips which left the welts had latex in them. Previous strips used on me did not. Allergic reaction to latex is a recognised problem. When Baby John visited and I explained that there was latex in the strips that had caused the welts, he recalled that latex allergies were well documented in the US.

There were so many accoutrements attached to my care once the issue of my MRSA was out in the open that I requested that a separate trolley be organised against the wall for their use. Obviously, judging from the special nurse who was assigned to me, the disease was major. My friend Dana Wynter was distraught on my behalf. Since she had a relative with the same staph infection, she was able to tell me that in California, the only effective treatment for MRSA was Vancomycin. This wasn't available to me, and it was both frustrating and upsetting to know that someone outside the medical profession knew more about the cure for my ailment than the doctors treating me. Nothing hurt me as much in the Blackrock Clinic as the news from the Bel Air on 18 December that Fidelma Freeman's husband, Bill, had died the previous day without warning. Only three weeks earlier, that same Wednesday when I told Fidelma of my cancer, she and I had sat in the hotel lobby that evening with her friend, Anne, and I'd asked Fidelma to tell me about meeting Bill and their courtship. Anne filled in some good bits that Fidelma was leaving out about Bill, who came from the village of Inch in County Wexford. He was such a big man with such a handsome face that it was easy to visualise what a Clark Gable he'd been in his youth. That evening, as we three women laughed and talked, enjoying the hotel's renowned apple pie, Fidelma's concern was for me, because of my cancer news shared with her that morning.

More times than I could remember over the past nine years, I'd watched Bill Freeman descend the grand Victorian staircase in the Bel Air's lobby. He cut quite a figure surrounded by the dark, shiny mahogany. Taking one careful step, then another, he'd always pause a moment on the landing before carrying on down to the bottom. Then settling on his stool beside the reception desk, he'd be ready for a whisky and a chat. He took even greater care coming down after his hip replacement, and, aided by a cane, he'd head for the kitchen, no longer taking his stool beside reception. But for me he was still part of the Bel Air's magic, and I needed to see for myself that he was gone. Fortunately, Baby John, my friend from LA, having returned to Dublin from Limerick, offered to drive me to the hotel, where I perched on a top stair and sang for Bill's spirit while Fidelma and her four children sat and listened. Five weeks earlier, when I had sat where they were sitting, discussing Bill with Fidelma and her friend, Anne, my life was the one which had seemed endangered; five weeks later, Fidelma would be widowed and Bill would be a memory.

I was eager to leave the Blackrock Clinic, because having discovered that I had a potentially incurable infection, I knew that I could heal better on my own. Though I refused to give up my belief that I'd had a skin reaction due to the latex in the strips put on my breast wound, the Blackrock Clinic's allergist said I'd tested negative. I checked out on 23 December. My actor friend, Tom Hickey, had arrived to drive me to the Bel Air. But our first stop was Macken's Pharmacy, where I went with the prescription that Arnie had given me for Zyvox and Cyproxin. These tablets were meant to heal me of MRSA. I knew I'd be safer in my Bel Air chalet, where I pinned the Blackrock's printout about MRSA on the side table next to the sofa so that I could remember the words methicillin-resistant Staphylococcus aureus.

The sound of my feet dragging across the floor in the black satin Chinese slippers that Eithne Mulherne had bought me is what made me realise how sick I was, that and the fact that I barely shifted from the sofa. The distance from it to the ground-floor bathroom was barely ten paces, yet I was grateful that I rarely needed the toilet, because getting up to walk was such an effort. In spite of how badly I felt, there were no symptoms that described my illness. I couldn't claim a stomach ache or headache, had no nausea, no fever, nor diarrhoea, and the only pain I could describe was that it felt like a horse had kicked me in the area around my infected wound. My energy level was below zero.

I'd hear myself sigh and moan and realise that I was often wringing my hands, but I sensed that not discussing my ill health was the only way to get well.

'How are you?' friends asked when they rang, but as they were rushing around getting ready for Christmas, nobody needed to hear that I felt too ill to explain.

'Great,' I'd say and be glad to get off the phone so that I could lie staring at the ceiling until the phone rang again to force me to repeat that I felt fine.

Deborah McNaughton was one of the few I'd tell exactly how I felt, because I hoped that it would encourage her to be as honest about how she was now that her breast cancer had metastasised into other organs. Mostly we kept in touch with cheerful e-mails, and I knew that all she could think about as Christmas Day grew nearer was her deceased lover, Noel Redding, who would have been 60 that December, were he still living. A couple of times when I rang her in Santa Fe, I could hear in her voice that she was sicker than she admitted. But maybe she'd hang up and say the same thing about me.

Long ago I gave up watching television, because it makes me a watcher rather than a liver, so the TV sat unplugged in the corner of the room, its grey screen reflecting not much more than the light from the living-room windows.

Snow fell on Christmas morning. As it came down in big white flakes, I got a lot of joy singing a few rounds of 'White Christmas' before Christine brought Stefan and his father, Nick, to see me after they'd been to church. But in truth, I was only two days out of the hospital and could barely muster the pretence of caring about the festivities. Normally as Christmas approaches, I head for la montagne, where I can avoid the commercial insanity. That's not to say that I do no gift giving. Nothing is nicer than giving people you love a gift that you know they'll enjoy, even if it's something crazy like the huge ham I gave Christine, because she's a great hostess. Sometimes I give things that are mine and that I really treasure. For instance, the octogenarian actress, Marsha Hunt, who modelled during the Second World War, produced a wonderful coffee-table book called *The Way We Wore*, featuring her in remarkable clothes. She gave me a copy, signing it, 'from Marsha Hunt I to Marsha Hunt II'. Kathy loves clothes and I knew she'd adore this big book. As snow continued to fall on that Christmas of 2004, I drove higher into the mountains, heading first for Kathy and Paul's. They asked me to stay, but I insisted that I move on, as I was just as determined to deliver gifts to the Doyles, who had been equally good to me. To see Marie and Ted with their three children, including Majella, the young surgeon who had found Arnie Hill for me, put the Christ in Christmas.

III

Love in my Gloves

*Words are things, and a small drop of
ink falling like dew upon a thought
produces that which makes thousands,
perhaps millions, think.*

LORD BYRON

15

Icon

There's a great photograph on the wall of the bedroom where I sleep at the Prebbles' of Marilyn Prebble made up and posed to look like a young Lauren Bacall. What's curious is that as soon as I saw the photo, I knew who it was meant to be. I've only seen Lauren Bacall in a couple of movies, but her young page-boy image is so familiar that it was obvious to me who Marilyn's lookalike shot is meant to be. It was taken in Newcastle in the late '70s when she was still modelling. She's blonder now, still looks great, and don't ask why I call her Marzipan, but I've clung to that ghetto thing of nicknaming people.

Marzipan, as I've earlier mentioned, is Stuart Prebble's wife. I guess he deserves her as much as any man deserves the perfect homemaker. She keeps both their homes immaculate, spoils their adult daughter, Alex, as well as every guest that crosses their threshold. She draws and paints with flourish, forgets no one's birthday and makes cooking a three-course meal look easy. Maybe it was the years of caring for their daughter, Sammi, who died of cystic fibrosis aged 16, that makes Marzipan a carer right down to her cuticles, or maybe she came into the world that way. On 6 January when she came to my rescue, I was doing a lookalike photo, and the idea for it may have come from seeing her lookalike pose of Lauren Bacall.

In December, I'd suggested to Stuart that we ask Patrick Lichfield to photograph me after my mastectomy to replicate the well-known shot he took of me for American *Vogue* after *Hair*'s opening night in '68. As I've already said, that black-and-white nude photo of me with a huge afro has cropped up so often during the past 37 years that it seems to have a life of its own.

When the photo session with Patrick was scheduled for 6 January, five weeks after my mastectomy, I imagined I'd be up and running by then. What I hadn't planned on was getting MRSA or the intensive antibiotic treatment that I endured trying to cure it. So when I flew to London on 5 January to spend the night with the Prebbles in Kingston, those heavy antibiotics that I'd been on for three weeks may have had more to do with how badly I was feeling than my mastectomy or the MRSA, which Arnie Hill believed I was clear of. Though I had managed the plane ride after my 90-minute drive from the Bel Air to Dublin airport, I was as sick as a dog.

I was neither nauseous nor hot with fever, but the right side of my chest, the site of my operation, felt as though some heavyweight had given me a going over, and my energy and spirit were so depleted that I was a stranger to myself. Relieved that Stuart and Marzipan couldn't break a long-standing dinner date, I fell into bed early only to find that lying down felt almost worse than sitting up. By the following morning, I was feeling so weak that I leapt at Marzipan's offer to come with Stuart and me to the filming of Patrick's photo session. I knew if I started to unravel, she'd be there to rescue me.

In the taxi delivering the three of us to the Lichfield Studios in Notting Hill, I would have crumpled in the seat had I been alone. Instead, I sat up laughing and talking, because that's what Stuart and Marzipan are used to. My silence is for France, where for days on end I might not speak. But this was London, and, thanks to my bright idea, I had a shoot on during which I wasn't only going to be photographed but also going to be filmed being photographed. Thankfully, my brown skin camouflaged how pale I was feeling, and as I was claiming that I felt fine, I had to live up to it.

The great thing about years in show business is that I was well rehearsed in 'the show must go on' and had performed ill too many times to remember, so it seemed in no way extraordinary that, while I was feeling like hell, I was about to be filmed doing a nude photo session with Patrick Lichfield.

When the taxi pulled up in front of his studio, Stuart's small film crew was ready and waiting. Marzipan stayed in the cab until they had filmed a couple of takes of me entering the building, then followed me in. To hear her say, 'Don't worry, I'll take your bag,' was a reminder that she was my blessing for the day, because while I would normally insist on carrying my own bag, at that moment I needed all the help that I could get.

I think the last time that I had seen Patrick Lichfield was in 1973, when he was a guest on my Capital Radio live late-night talk show. In the studio with us were the film actor Oliver Reed and the fashion photographer David Bailey. With hindsight, I'd say that when our discussion moved on to playboys, my prying into their exploits would now have some feminists on the warpath. Oliver Reed, for one, who was then one of Britain's top leading men, liked his drink and was a notorious womaniser.

After all those years, Patrick had hardly changed. His head of thick hair, cut as it was then, was now grey, and there were so few lines on his handsome face that I joked about cosmetic surgery.

It's his title rather than his easy manner that tells you he's first cousin to the Queen. To be greeted by his smile and charming compliments made me feel that it had been weeks rather than decades since we'd worked together.

When we last time did a session together in November of '69, I was a little overwhelmed, because Diana Vreeland, the fashion doyenne and editor of American *Vogue*, had chosen me to be the first black face on the cover and flown me back to London to shoot it with Patrick. Though I was a London-based rock singer, I had been in Copenhagen working on my first movie. The pictures that Patrick took of me never graced *Vogue*'s cover, but neither of us forgot that we'd come so near.

During the summer of 2004, his National Portrait Gallery exhibition had included the nude of me in '68, which the gallery had reproduced as a postcard. Now here I was, a single-breasted granny, back to replicate that image.

This second time around was very different, because what made the original morning session so memorable was how little fuss was made to get the picture. I did my hair and make-up, Patrick had one assistant, and of the two others at the session, one was Pamela Colin, the editor in London of American *Vogue*. She was then a New Yorker, but had since married Lord Harlech.

This time there was a crowd, including Stuart and his film crew, the five who work for Patrick and a make-up lady whom the studio had booked to duplicate my make-up from 1968. Taking one look at me, she must have known she'd have a job making me look less glassy-eyed.

In the studio dressing-room, Marzipan was busy hanging the clothes I'd brought and said, 'You dropped this.'

My mouth dropped open when I saw what she was holding. I

snatched it. 'Christ! That crumby thing! Wash your hands!'

'It was on the pavement. You must have dropped it getting out of the cab . . .'

'Oh lord, Marilyn, wash them good!' I pointed to the sink behind her.

That flesh-coloured square had touched my breast wound.

Not only had I rejected the option of breast reconstruction, I also refused to wear the false breast given to me free as part of my treatment at St Vincent's Private. They had fitted me with a free bra that had a cup with a pocket, into which went the false breast, called a prosthesis.

'I'm not wearing that,' I'd told the breast-care nurse. I'll get some clothes that will look OK with a single breast. I wanted nothing that would make me feel that having only one breast was abnormal. Because one breast was now normal for me, and my bras had to accommodate the missing breast. Cutting out the right cup and sewing together the remaining fabric so that it was flat wasn't hard, but I'm no seamstress. To hide the bad finish, I stuck on a special three-inch-by-three-inch adhesive bandage provided by the hospital to cover my wound.

To discover that Marzipan had picked up the bandage struck me like hearing that she'd handled an infected syringe. So horrified was I that I had to sit down, and after she'd washed her hands, I did the same.

Stuart popped his head in the door. 'Mind if the cameraman comes in while you're getting made up?'

'Course not,' I lied with a smile. What I really wanted was to crawl in a ball on the floor, and maybe Marzipan knew.

'All right, pet? What can I do?'

Sometimes just to hear somebody offer help and know that the person means it is all that's needed. Not since I'd left the Blackrock Clinic had I had help from anyone. Though I took pride in my independence, there were times when I badly needed help. The day of the photo session was one. Marzipan hung just close enough that she was always there to be leaned on but never so close to be in the way. And I thought about how she must have learned the subtlety of that in the loving care she gave to Sammi. But maybe it was also the fact that Marzipan had been a model and knew that somebody helping you on and off with a dress, finding your underpants, fetching the hairpins and boosting your confidence by saying that you looked great just before you stepped out in front of the camera was better than a guardian angel.

She was there in the dressing-room when I'd washed my hands and noticed while drying them that the skin, particularly on the right one, was peeling off. I stared at them and rushed them to the light; it was like something from a horror movie. Somehow, since the last time I'd noticed my hands, they'd begun to peel, like they were recovering from a bad sunburn, and there I was with a studio filled with people waiting to examine me.

I hissed, 'Marzipan! Marzipan!'

'What, pet?' She was a few feet away, quietly perched on the edge of a tall stool, and six feet away was the pert make-up artist putting away her make-up.

'Look at my hands!' I whispered, hoping the make-up girl couldn't hear. 'See . . . look! The bloody skin's coming off!' Was this a sign that MRSA – methicillin-resistant Staphylococcus aureus – was still in my bloodstream? And what would start peeling next? Was my whole body going to peel? That potentially fatal infection with its ability to attack the heart and the brain made me wary of what to expect next.

The beautiful black-and-red hand-printed velvet shawl that Marie Doyle had given me for Christmas was perfect for getting me from the dressing-room to the shoot, and two steps behind, uttering that all-time booster phrase, 'Don't you look fabulous?'

was the tall, blonde, dimpled Marzipan, looking way more ready for the cameras than I was.

In Patrick's studio, which is a huge voluptuous space, with so many present and watching, it felt more like acting on a movie set than what I remembered of the quiet intimacy of the original session. Back then I had wanted to please Patrick, because he was the eye of the camera. And he had said all those encouraging things that I recall all photographers used to say to models, like 'That's beautiful', 'Fantastic, darling', 'Hold it there, that's sensational', 'Just move to your right . . . yes that's perfect', 'Perfect', 'Eyes to me', 'Now give me a smile', 'Part your lips just a little', 'Yes!', 'Nice' – and even the little pockets of silence were sensual, because this guy was so focused upon you and you were there to please his eye. It was intimate, sexual, provocative.

Thirty-seven years later, it was quite different. Now, with polaroids, digital cameras, computers and screens, it's more of a technical operation, and happy though I was to see Patrick and vice versa, we were both aware of being filmed and could make no more than a superficial connection, although I'm sure he's not a superficial man. He strikes me as patrician, as one who has seen a great deal and continues to take an interest in interesting things. I don't doubt that we could have had an intereting conversation about nudity and breasts, had there been time. But there wasn't.

Though the MRSA infection had made my wound unsightly, I wasn't the least bit embarrassed about it. This was now me, and what you see is what you get. A couple of times while Patrick and his assistant were checking shots on the computer screen a few feet away, I shouted to Marzipan, 'How're we looking? Is my hair OK?'

'Fabulous, pet.'

What lies behind us and what lies before us are tiny matters compared to what lies within us.

RALPH WALDO EMERSON

16

Forgive Us Our Trespasses

When my BlackBerry buzzed at five minutes to five to say I had mail, I was alone. I wasn't sick but nor was I well. It was dark out, 11 January, which was a Tuesday, and I'd drawn the drapes to keep out the cold. A roaring peat fire in the open stove cast a glow, and in the left corner of the red sofa facing it, as usual, I sat propped up by cushions and surrounded by the bits and pieces that let me avoid moving. The phone, my mobile, a small CD player, my laptop, iPod and BlackBerry were all within arm's reach.

The BlackBerry buzzed several times a day, and I always grabbed it with anticipation. It was that element of surprise coupled with the absence of intrusion that made it so much better than the phone. I needed to exert no energy, feign no pleasantness, pretend no interest, offer no response. And if I squinted, I didn't even need my glasses to read the text. But that Tuesday, my glasses were perched on the end of my nose when I tapped the icon which opens the mail.

The e-mail read, 'From: Clare Turner. Subject: On behalf of Mick Jagger.'

I'd never heard of Clare Turner, but it began, 'Hello, Marsha'. She explained that she was contacting me from Prince Rupert Lowenstein's office. That instantly raised my guard. His name had figured in my life between 1978 and 1988 when his merchant bank in London issued the paltry payments I received from Mick after taking him to court for the second time to supplement the 500 pounds per year previously paid towards our daughter's welfare. As I associated the name Prince Rupert Lowenstein with those ten silly financial years, this e-mailer's association with him did her no good. But aware that Rupert now worked for the Rolling Stones, I read on, not surprised that Clare mentioned Sherry Daly's name.

At that stage, I thought Sherry was Keith Richards' secretary at the Stones' office. I liked her, and on my kitchen table, the elegant planter of white and mauve orchids which she'd sent to me at the hospital on his behalf were thriving. Clare said that I could ring Sherry to confirm that Clare was who she said she was and that Sherry would have introduced her, but Sherry's e-mail had gone down.

Holding the BlackBerry in my right hand, and using my thumb to scroll down the message, I got to the bit that said, 'Mick has asked me to make a bank transfer to your bank account.' More sentences followed; my mind froze there. However well intentioned this gesture, a turd of shit dropped through my letterbox would have been no less upsetting. A history that I thought I'd long since dealt with and buried was now here, staring me in the face. With my jaws tightly clenched, I was speechless. Had I been capable of sound, it would have been an excruciating roar heard for miles. But only the fire roared.

One measly line from a stranger on my BlackBerry provoked all the rage that I'd suppressed for decades related to Mick and his denial of me and our beloved daughter. Through critical years of her childhood and my career, whatever he had done to her, he'd also defamed me, when my income, like his, was dependent upon my public image and popularity.

Scrolling further down Clare's e-mail, it said that either I could call her with my bank details or e-mail them. Recommending that I split the information between two e-mails, she closed with, 'Many thanks, Marsha. Kind regards, Clare Turner.'

'No you fucking don't!' I snapped, throwing off the shawl that covered my legs and prying myself from the sofa to go and make tea. I wanted something stronger, but five was too early to start drinking.

Making my way to the kettle at the far end of the kitchen, the sound of my slippered feet dragging across the stone floor reminded me that those two days in London, with flights there and back and the long drive to and from Dublin airport, had taken a heavy toll. I'd been back nearly a full five days and still hadn't the energy to unpack my bag, which remained in the downstairs bedroom.

At times like these, being alone was no good. I needed a sounding board, but who'd understand my anger? Who wouldn't say take the money and run, knowing how much I owed Karis and my old friend, Steve Lovi in San Francisco, not to mention the AIB bank and Kathy. On the table beside the planter of orchids was the Christmas card which she'd discreetly handed me in an envelope at her port party ten days earlier, saying 'Put that somewhere safe.' I'd reluctantly accepted the 5,000-euro cheque inside, not only because I badly needed it but because I also needed to learn to accept help from friends who offered it.

Money. Money. Money. Money. Money. Money. Money. Money.

Had this been a scene in a movie, that O'Jays R 'n' B classic 'Money' could have phased in as background music. But this was real life, and my indignation about a strange woman e-mailing me from Rupert's office on Mick's behalf had me revving up to rail. What rankled was that I believed that my income continued to suffer because of the cloud that hung over my name due to him. Did I now have to let him be the nice guy without him so much as having to lift the phone to me?

A month earlier when I'd asked Mick to find me the name of the best allergist in Dublin, I'd felt so helpless on my back in that hospital bed that I'd blown my cool and cried. He didn't ring back for days, so when Steph Lawrence, his secretary, eventually rang to ask where to send my Christmas gift, the poor girl got an outburst meant for him. But the sweet joy of our grandson's birth didn't let me stay angry for long. Without Mick there would have been no Zach, no Mazie, no Karis.

Despite having so many friends, there are few with whom I'd discuss a problem related to Mick. He's such an icon that I've noticed even the most intelligent, learned people can't always see that he is merely a man. Their judgement is affected by admiration for his talent and success, his public profile, the well-established photo images of him, his singing, or, worse, the peculiar notion that he is someone they know. For some, his fame has made him part of their consciousness. For me, he is in my life, and that e-mail meant he was suddenly in my face.

By the time I rang Bassam Alghanim, I'd already spoken to two girlfriends who both said, 'Take the money.' Sam, as I call him, has got so much, he can afford to see beyond it. I was looking for somebody who sympathised with my intention to turn it down.

'How much is it, Missy?' was his first question.

'Fucked if I know. Why d'you ask?'

I could hear him taking a drag on his cigarette. His gift is that he spots and enjoys the comedy in life. 'You want to turn down money and don't know how much you're turning down?' He had such a good laugh about that, that I started laughing myself, and as soon as I did, my anger shifted, and I somewhat calmed down. Though it was ten in the morning in LA and the business day had started, Bassam was still enjoying a winter break. Being a banker with his own bank, money is business, and he's unemotional about it. The beauty of our long friendship is that I neither hold him in contempt for being rich nor does he denigrate me for being broke. He has ways of helping me help myself, like the new Apple laptop and digital camera he got me for Christmas, and in November, when I rang to say I had cancer, he said, 'Anything you need, sweetie, you got.'

So far, I'd needed nothing but advice.

Baby John Ladner had seen me weeks earlier, known me since we were 18, and dealt with the likes of Prince Rupert when Rupert and John acted as Karis's trustees. Though this gave John real insight into my dilemma, having seen me in hospital he knew that I was more fragile than I claimed. He said, 'You do need money.'

'But not from him. What? Somebody breaks your kneecaps, you spend your life crawling, and maybe when you've reached the end of the line, he sends crutches?'

John's years on the bench give him the edge on making judgements. 'But . . .'

I didn't want to hear any buts. 'If I take money from him now, I'll be compromised about what I can say in my Jimi book. Mick does figure in this little history.'

'OK,' said John. 'I didn't know that was a factor.'

This man, whom I often call Michael, to distinguish him from the Rolling Stones icon that he's become, is bonded for ever into my small family through my daughter and her children, who mean everything to me. For their sake, I had forgiven whatever I rightly or wrongly held against him. And for their sake, although I couldn't accept Michael's charity, offered in an e-mail by a third party, to decline it had to be done graciously.

By 6.30 p.m., I'd decided that a glass of wine half an hour earlier than usual didn't make me an alcoholic, and after sticking a few more briquettes of peat on the fire, I settled back on the sofa, ready, or so I thought, for another winter's night. But that e-mail from Clare Turner had my mind working overtime. Cancer. Sickness. Life and Death and all that biblical stuff about Christ's forgiveness: had I forgiven Michael or was I kidding myself? While I lay there questioning my motives for rejecting his money or my right to, I started feeling angry that he'd disturbed my peace when I needed it most. One thing I was positive about with healing is that you have to do it both physically and mentally, both inside and out. Anxiety, anger, upset: I had no time for any of it. But while I sat there sipping red wine, my blood was boiling and I felt angry and tormented.

'Stop this. Will you stop?' I chastised myself. 'Put this to bed.'

Easier said than done. By the time I went up to bed myself, I thought I'd come up with an acceptable plan.

The next day, Mick was in LA for the Golden Globe

awards, as he'd been nominated with Dave Stewart for the title song that they'd written for the remake of *Alfie*.

After I'd e-mailed Clare Turner to say I'd be pleased if the bank transfer went to Karis, I was ready to let the issue rest. She e-mailed me back to say that Mick wanted to talk to me, but, of course, that was the last I heard about the mess.

The world is not respectable; it is mortal tormented, confused, deluded forever; but it is shot through with beauty, with love, with glints of courage and laughter; and in these, the spirit blooms.

GEORGE SANTAYANA

17

Hairless in Hollywood

Though losing my hair through chemotherapy was of no importance to me, letting my granddaughter see the process of my becoming bald was. I can't say why I sensed that it would be important to our friendship. Maybe it had something to do with that moment in August when I had Mazie in the wheelbarrow under the stars, and she said confidentially, 'Karis's mother has long, long hair,' coupled with her excitement the following day when she saw me with my hair down.

Karis agreed that it would be good for Mazie and some of Mazie's little pals to join in cutting my hair and see me become bald, and from that kernel of a notion blossomed the hair-cutting party. Being only three, Mazie wasn't yet told of my plan, because there remained the possibility that I wouldn't shake my MRSA infection. For many, the Staphylococcus aureus gets a grip and holds on. It can kill. My determination to get to LA for a hair-cutting party made me take my Zyvox and Cyproxin tablets on time. I also tended my infected breast wound with clinical precision and avoid anyone with a cold. It's also why 12 January

2005 was benchmarked as such an important day in my life. It's the day that the oncologist, Dr John McCaffrey, was to ring me with the results of my MRSA tests taken at the Mater Private Hospital.

If the results were negative and I no longer had the infection, not only could I book my flight to LA but Dr McCaffrey could also schedule my six months of chemotherapy treatments at the Mater Private.

That Wednesday the 12th, by late afternoon, I was still on tenterhooks waiting for the test results when I walked into Avoca Handweavers, a store south of Dublin in County Wicklow, to meet up with Alan, who was to give me some tapes that we'd filmed while I was sick and angry in the hospital. To have him contribute his gifts as a documentary film-maker to my cause was more than I could ever thank him for. More than once he'd arrived with his camera equipment to film what I would have trusted no other living soul to shoot.

Prior to his cancer, when we'd lived together in the Wicklow Mountains, Avoca Handweavers had been one of our coffee stops, and it remained convenient, because the Bel Air wasn't far and Alan and his wife, Catherine, had bought a house nearby. At holiday time, the store is a gathering hole for tourists, amongst others, because its Irish goods range from soap and crockery to clothing, books and soda bread. It attracts shoppers who have that well-heeled organic vegetarian look: *Guardian* readers in expensive bulky knits and sensible leather shoes. The cafeteria, which caters for them, is always crowded.

That Wednesday, as I stepped in from the cold, the after-Christmas sale had the place crawling with women who lunch wearing country tweeds and just a hint of make-up. Since Alan had just rung my mobile to say he was running late, I figured I'd pass the time browsing in the book section and as I headed for it, an older woman, small and Irish, caught my eye and made a beeline for me.

I found myself backed in a corner, when she said, 'You're Marsha who was with Mick Jagger, aren't you? Did you see Jerry Hall on telly the other night? He should've stuck with you . . . You look way better than her, you do.' She'd no intention of moving on.

Over the years, my various professions – singing, acting, radio presenting and writing books – have made me as much public property as a park bench. Though I've learned to tolerate it, imagine perfect strangers wanting to discuss your family business. As Mick's wife for 20 years, Jerry had been Karis's stepmother, and a nice one. To have to put up with comparisons being made between us by a stranger in a store was not on, and being in Ireland, I was willing to wager that this little commentator penning me in knew at least one person that I did.

Moving in closer, she smiled. 'I read that book you wrote about your grandmother. What was it called . . .'

'*Repossessing Ernestine,*' I smiled back, trying to be pleasant. 'Did you enjoy it?'

'Did you see Jerry?' she harped, 'On *The Late Late* . . .'

'My grandmother lived on to be 103,' I said to change the subject.

'He should have stuck with you,' said the little woman, looking for my agreement and beckoning a dark-haired young woman who approached just as I spotted Alan from afar, coming through the glass doors.

'Mum,' said the younger woman, 'I've been looking for you. C'mon. Let's . . .'

'This is Marsha,' her mother chirped, turning to introduce us as though I was an old school chum. 'Oooh, and is this your fella?' she beamed, just as Alan reached us. Women of all ages are quick to make a fuss of him, because apart from being tall and handsome, his years as an athlete have left him with that clean-cut jock look. As we'd lived together for four years, such situations were old hat, and, aware that I'd been cornered by a stranger, he exchanged a courteous hello with the two women and instantly freed me from the spot.

'Hey, Bear,' I greeted him, initially grateful for a getaway, but it took only one look at his eyes to see that he was poorly. 'You OK?' I asked as we settled at small table for two in a far corner of the cafeteria near the back exit.

'Flu. Been in bed.'

'Flu!' I yelped, almost leaping from my chair. 'And what, you come out to give me the flu?! Are you crazy! I'm just getting over MRSA! And you know I'm trying to get to LA. If I catch the flu, my ass could end up back in the hospital.'

'Keep your voice down, Bunny.'

Ex-boyfriends. With the way he whispers and wants me to whenever we're out, anybody would think we were exchanging state secrets.

I said, 'Dr McCaffrey's meant to be calling me with the results of my MRSA tests. He promised to let me know today whether I can fly to LA. If I catch the flu . . .'

John McCaffrey had not only been Alan's oncologist at the Mater Private Hospital but during the five subsequent years, he'd continued to see Alan for his six-monthly check-ups. The quality of Dr McCaffrey's care, along with that of the radiologist, Dr Michael Maher, was the incentive that made me return to the hospital for my post-cancer treatment.

Days before Christmas, Dr McCaffrey's acceptance of me as his patient had allowed me to relax, knowing that, whatever happened, I was now with a medical team and hospital which I'd got to know when I was both healthy myself and judicious on

Alan's behalf. Whether it was the fourth-floor cancer ward, the chapel, the cafeteria or the little newspaper kiosk which had carried my prison book, the place had been my stomping ground. From July '99 through January 2000, a chat with the hospital priest or a 'good morning' or 'good night' to the security guards and the receptionists who manned the front desk made me no stranger to the Mater Private's staff.

In Avoca Handweavers' cafeteria, while Alan and I discussed Dr McCaffrey, he rang my mobile. I was so anxious to hear his every word that I shifted from the restaurant to the children's clothing section. I was standing under the pink net angel costumes when he said, 'You're clear of the MRSA, and we'd like to bring you in on 30 January to start your chemotherapy.'

'And it's OK to book my flight to LA?'

Nobody could have imagined how lucky I felt to be driving Tim Curry's new silver Merc down Sunset Boulevard on Sunday, 23 January. It wasn't just that Tim, who was in New York rehearsing for a new Broadway musical, gave me the use of his house and car, it was that I'd managed to be in LA at all for the five-day jaunt. I thought it unfair and unwise to stay at Karis's with her breast feeding the new baby, but after 36 hours in town, plans for the Tuesday hair-cutting party were set. My close friend Bassam Alghanim not only offered to supply the champagne but he was also going to have Martin, his French-Canadian chef, cater the lunch-time gathering for 20 at Karis's.

That Sunday I was driving down Sunset to meet her, Jonathan, Mazie, the new baby and Mick for lunch at the Bel Air Hotel, where Mick was a guest. My Bel Air Hotel and his in Bel Air, just west of Beverly Hills, couldn't have been more opposite. His is five star, as was Sunday's weather. When a Bel Air car hop opened my door and exchanged my car keys for a parking ticket,

I stepped out to the embrace of the warm California sun and the scent of the Bel Air's lush gardens.

When I'd last seen Mick at the hotel, it was the day after we'd witnessed Mazie's birth, and he'd asked me to join him, his girlfriend, L'Wren, and three of his associates for lunch on his 58th birthday. Now, three years on, six-week-old Zach was our new family addition and Mazie was playing the proud big sister.

Early that morning, she and I had been having scissor practice with some I'd bought especially for little hands. With an open mouth, I watched her trying to cut paper, and when her cutting method didn't work, she tore off whatever paper remained stuck in the scissors. Of course, I was imagining her going at my hair, although she didn't know about my cockamamie notion that she could be the barber at my hair-cutting party, now two days away.

'Baby Girl,' I said as torn bits of paper mounted up, 'it'd be easier if you use that other finger. Want Grammy to show you?' I guessed her answer would be no even before she said so.

That she was descended from a long line of female warriors was often apparent, even on minor issues such as what shoes she'd wear or when to get out of the pool. 'Stubborn' was her mother's take on it, but I considered it a genetic trait. Whatever seeded Mazie's will, that Sunday-morning scissor practice, as she concentrated and was having a cutting good time, it seemed unwise to show her that the middle finger was more effective than the index for cutting. Sure, it put my dream of her cutting my hair to rest, but I was nonetheless glad that I'd come, so she would witness the process.

Later that afternoon, during Sunday lunch at the Bel Air, when she sat beside me at the round table with her grandfather, Mick, across from her and her parents side by side with her baby brother, I took a few snaps, to preserve the memory for her of this pretty little family gathering under a canopy with the crystal goblets, pink linen napkins and delicate posy. While cancer had sharpened my sense of how fragile and fleeting human life may be, that sunny January afternoon we were three generations strong, proof of life's resilient power.

Two afternoons later, I hoped that the lunch-time gathering for the hair-cutting party was going to be equally memorable for Mazie. In addition to my hair being cut, it was a chance to celebrate my friend, Enid Graddis's, 60th birthday. But I wanted to remember the real purpose of this party was to establish for Mazie that neither my losing a breast nor my baldness due to cancer were things to be puzzled about.

Seeing her mother breast feeding Zach informed Mazie of the breasts' vital function in providing milk for her baby brother, and it seemed equally important for her to know that women can be healthy and happy with one breast or none. I'd therefore asked Karis's permission to let Mazie see my amputation that morning, so that she could witness that having one breast hadn't changed me. I didn't make a big deal about it but caught her eye while I was slipping my T-shirt off in the den. 'Wanna see Grammy's scar? I had a big operation and it didn't even hurt. Grammy was brave.' Though she took a quick look, she was far more interested in the DVD she was watching.

Karis and Jonathan's house in Laurel Canyon was the perfect setting for a gathering which included a couple of Mazie's friends as well as some of mine and Karis's. With the long stretch of glass walls and sliding glass door overlooking the pool and patio with its cactus garden, the hilltop houses across the canyon enhanced the panorama. The only thing missing that sunny afternoon was Jonathan, who, as a first assistant director on a big-budget movie shooting out at Universal, couldn't get home to join the party.

The sound of champagne bottles popping throughout the delicious buffet lunch which Bassam's staff laid out added to the sense of occasion even before I brought out the big candlelit birthday cake for Enid. But by the time I sat by the fireplace to braid and cut my hair, I realised that a glass of champagne too many meant I wouldn't be up to speed when braiding my hair to make the cutting quicker.

'This could take me ages,' I announced to the gathered, who had collected in the living room to watch. 'Anybody here know how to braid?' There was a moment's silence before all the women were chiming, 'I know', 'I can', 'Course I can braid'. And before I knew what was happening, six of them had rushed over, arranged themselves in a semicircle and got their hands working on my hair. Despite their sophisticated clothes and French perfumes, their professionally manicured hands and feet, their chatter and laughter brought to mind a tribe of native women busy weaving while the men stood watching, with their asides and banter, and the kids ran around barefoot.

To be the centre of this hubbub was comical but also touching, because, collectively, a couple of hundred years of friendship were busy at my hair. Opposite Karis was Big Charis, from whom I took Karis's name, although I'd spelled it differently. When Charis Horton and I became friends during the summer of '64, we were Berkeley freshmen. The only one in the room who'd known me longer was my brother, Dennis. Braiding beside Karis was Andrea Luria, also an ol' Berkeley buddy, whose friendship had endured for 40 years, and next to her was Sheila Scott Wilkinson, whom I'd known since our *Hair* rehearsals in London in '68. Though I'd only known Ione Skye, the movie actress, since she and Karis became friends in '77, they were only six at that time, which meant that I'd known Ione for most of her life and her mother, Enid, for as many years. All tolled, that was 173 years, with Karis's adding 34 more to the load.

After this busy braiding brigade turned my long, bushy mane into a mass of neat, fat plaits, Bassam suggested that we'd better secure either end with rubber bands, and Karis miraculously produced a pack of coloured ones. When all was done, I sat on the chair grinning like a Cheshire cat, though I was looking more like a black Medusa.

Being lunch time, several people present, including my journalist brother, Dennis, had jobs to return to that afternoon. The Oscar nominations were being announced, and he was anxious to get to Universal. To have him antsy at my side, bearing the scissors, so reminded me of our childhood, when he, being three years older, always seemed to be rushing me. But still I howled, 'Mazie first!' and, thankfully, Enid was there to give her a hand with the scissors.

As the first braid was cut and held high like a talisman for all to see, a great whoop went up from the whole group. From that moment on, there was such a sense of a communal ceremony that I felt blessed that this attention was all for me. With everyone, including Mazie's three-year-old friends, Miles and Kate, taking turns, I had no time for even a tinge of regret as the braids piled up on the coffee table, with hoots and hollers to grace each. Instead, I was relieved and happy that what could have been a failed event had all the makings of a jubilee, with the highlight for me being when someone asked the three kids if they knew why my hair was being cut. They were standing together within arm's reach of me when Miles piped in, both assured, yet a little hesitant, 'Grammy's got to take some medicine and she . . . her hair . . .'

I dare not quote the rest. I couldn't do justice to his baby intent on relating the facts, with some interjections from Mazie, as Ione's little girl, the wide-eyed Kate, looked on. For me, this is what it was all about, the children's comprehension and lack of fear about my having had cancer and its side effects.

When Miles's mother, Fabienne Toback, produced the shears that she'd brought from home, I needed a volunteer to shave the hair that remained, as I shifted out to the patio with another glass of champagne. Though Bassam's house guest, Hassan Shuman, visiting from Beirut and just learning English, was a little shy of taking part, he soon became the star of the hour when he admitted that he was used to shaving heads.

'Head down, please . . . head back.'

With the sun on my face, an orange towel to protect my shoulders, the buzz of the shears in my ears and an audience of good friends, I tried hard to sit still while thick clumps of what hair remained fell to the ground.

'How's he doing?' I asked Bassam, who was intently studying the procedure.

'You've got a perfect head, Missy.'

'It looks great,' chimed in Enid, the birthday girl, who was standing beside him. The barefoot Mazie, who'd crouched down beside me, seemed less curious about my hair than what the bald-headed Hassan was doing to it.

As Sheila from *Hair* days kept reminding people, 'Marsha did a Sinead O'Connor way before Sinead O'Connor.' But that was 1972, I was still in the rock and roll business and having my big afro shorn at Leonard's for *Vogue* was a fashion statement rather than cancer-related.

Most of the guests had gone by the time Mick arrived with Jade, her two pretty daughters, Sisi and Amba, her boyfriend, Dan, and his ten-year-old son, and my shaven head was no longer a novelty. It was only when Dan, who was meeting me for the first time, asked, 'What'd'you look like before?' that it struck home that I was about to hear this repeatedly.

After they nibbled at what was left of the buffet, I grabbed the digital camera that Bassam gave me for Christmas and asked Mick to pose with Karis, Jade and their kids on the sofa. It was a comforting sight, this collection of people whom I knew Karis, Mazie and Zach would have in their lives were I to move on. Yet, it was equally strange for me that having raised Karis alone, she was now the beloved eldest, the sensitive, sensible one of a large group of siblings and half-siblings. Jade's two daughters, both of whom she'd helped to deliver, loved her and she them. So I was genuinely pleased that I had a reason to take my leave. I had promised Big Charis that we'd have an early supper and I'd spend the night. I wanted a good long one-to-one, because we hadn't had a chance to spend time together since her husband, Antoine, had died of cancer in 2001.

When Mick carried my overnight bag out to Tim's car, I waved at Mick's English driver, Clive, who was parked in a limo across the street, then I kissed Mick on the cheek and began, 'Listen, Michael, about that money . . .'

We'd yet to talk about why he'd asked Clare Turner to transfer an undisclosed amount to my account and why I refused it, and I thought he deserved an explanation. 'There's never been money between us in all these years, so why start that now? If you want to do something nice for me, get Karis a new car. She can no doubt use a bigger one with the new baby.'

Michael Philip Jagger. Son of Eva Scutts Jagger and Basil Joe Jagger. Father of Karis and six who have followed her. This Michael, whom I had once loved enough to have his child, had produced a brood of which I was an outsider, though Karis and her children were a part. However angry he could make me, and no one was more capable of sending me into a blind rage, there would always be a morsel of love for Michael, because I'd raised a child who had his smile.

All nature is but art unknown to thee.
All chance, direction which thou
canst not see.

ALEXANDER POPE

18

Cancer Buddies

On Sunday, 29 January, when I checked into the Mater Private Hospital for two nights, I'd been back less than forty-eight hours after my whirlwind five days in LA. I couldn't believe that I had been assigned the same room that Alan had had back in '99 for his intensive week of chemotherapy. Having sat or stood by his bedside day after day, now, five years on, it was my turn in the bed while they kept a watch on how I responded to my first dose of chemo and checked me again for MRSA.

I'd brought very little apparel apart from a bright orange nightie of Karis's, an even brighter long red robe, black slippers and some black silk pyjamas. But as it's vital to my state of mind to make a hospital room my own, I'd also brought my little cushion which says, 'The best is yet to come', slung a long, glimmering scarf over the back of the bed, pinned a sheet of Mazie's artwork above it, posed my hand-painted cat bag on the shelf beside pictures of Karis's little family and arranged pink roses in a vase. When the nurse came to check my temperature and blood pressure, the room looked like I had been there for days. I was glad to be in bed early that Sunday night, because I knew that at nine the following morning, my documentary director, Eamon O'Connor, would be arriving with a cameraman and sound recorder to film me getting my first hit of chemo.

The nurses had predicted that I'd be sick within the first couple of hours, and although I knew a scene like that would make for good television, I hadn't vomited since 1970, just after being in labour with Karis. I wasn't looking forward to it.

Thankfully, at seven that Monday, as I frowned, gagged and bitched like a six year old as I tried to drink the foul-tasting two pints of solution required for that morning's CAT scan, the little film crew weren't yet around to catch me. But they did arrive in time to shoot me heading off for the elevator in my new red robe and black silk pyjamas, escorted by a young porter with a Dublin accent. As we made our way along the wide corridor that led to the elevators, since I wasn't a bit sick and certainly not doddery enough to warrant an escort down the X-ray department on the main floor, I told him, 'I'm happy to go by myself.' I was conscious of wasting the good time of a hospital employee who must have been needed elsewhere.

'I've got your file,' he said 'and we don't want you gettin' lost.'

We got in on the fourth floor. On the third, we were joined by a tall blond, also escorted by a porter. He was wearing black silk pyjamas. So was I. Mine were brand new. Bought on sale at Victoria's Secret in LA while I was there for the hair-cutting party. But his had seen a bit of wear. The deep black was slightly faded and the collar slightly dog-eared.

They had that lived-in look, as did his moccasin slippers, which were also well worn but of fine quality.

In that confined silvery elevator, I was aware of being alone with three men. Them silent and staring at their feet, and me dressed to be filmed, in full make-up – war paint, I call it – and painted toenails peeking out of my slinky black slippers. I looked more like I was decked out for a hot sexy romp in the sack than a boring full-body CAT scan.

At every step, possibly because I was in the same hospital where Alan had been a cancer patient back in '99, I was replaying situations that weren't exactly new to me. I'd been there as his carer, watching, cautious, anxious to do my best to make sure that he was getting the best. So in the elevator, I was remembering how I'd pushed Alan in a wheelchair down to the same X-ray department.

Although there were a couple of seats spare in the Mater Private's small X-ray department reception area, I find few things as annoying as sitting in a crowded reception with people almost shoulder to shoulder, so I made my way to the smaller section at the back, which was totally empty. As my porter headed in the opposite direction with my big file, I'd hardly arranged myself in my chair when the tall blond settled in the seat opposite, placing his leather briefcase on the floor by his feet. It was bulging with papers and looked even more weathered than his robe, black pyjamas and slippers.

Nothing seems sillier than two humans being in a small space pretending not to see each other, and what's trained me to do otherwise is having that writing studio in a rural French village where strangers always address each other and anyone entering a shop will hail, '*Bonjour, mesdames . . . messieurs.*'

Being American, I take it a little further, and so I said to the tall blond, 'We must be on the same team since we're both in the black silks.'

His laugh was hearty, and his 'You're right' had just that hint of an Irish lilt, as he answered his cell phone.

When he finished that first call, his mobile rang again.

'Kids,' he said after the second brief call.

'Yeah,' I agreed.

He stuck his phone in his robe pocket before picking up his bulging briefcase. He hadn't many lines on his face and could have been in his mid-40s, but the blond hair floating over the collar of his robe suggested that he was my generation. Nearly everyone waiting in the reception was dressed in street clothes. That he was an in-patient was a point of discussion.

'Been in long?' I asked.

'Just down for tests,' he said.

'Yeah. Me too. Arrived last night. Out tomorrow, thank God. Hospitals are dangerous places these days.'

'What have you got?'

'Had. Breast cancer. But that wasn't half as bad as the MRSA I got while I was in Vincent's Private.'

'My friend got that,' said the blond. And leaned over to whisper, 'In here. Terrible. He's been moved to a nursing home. No telling when he'll recover.'

'Sick as a dog, I was with it. Cancer was a doddle, but I thought the MRSA was going to take me out of here. And the real shocking thing is that nobody told me that I had it at St Vincent's Private. I wasn't told until I transferred into the Blackrock Clinic and a nurse kicked up about me walking the halls. I said to her, "Excuse me, I can walk where I want" and she said, "You've got MRSA and should stay in your room." I asked her how she was so sure and she said that it was on my records that came with me from St Vincent's. I was flabbergasted . . .'

When the nurse called my name, I said goodbye, checking that my BlackBerry was still in my pocket when I heard his phone ring again.

The waiting room that I was shown to had space for only three chairs. The door separating it from the room with the CAT scan machine had a high window. As I took a seat, I could hear the murmur of voices and hoped that with the Eamon and the crew waiting upstairs I wouldn't be kept too long.

The thought had barely passed through my mind when a nurse stuck her head out of the door to say she was sorry but the machine was down and there might be a wait.

'That's fine,' I told her as she stepped back into the CAT scan room before the tall blond man entered.

'Machine's down,' I said. He looked at his watch. 'You in a rush?'

'I was hoping to get on the road early. I'm driving to Clare.'

'Fuck. County Clare. That's a big drive.'

'I'm used to it. I live there.'

We spent more than an hour chatting in that room that was hardly more than a cubicle. By the time we said our goodbyes, he knew my name, I knew his was John Caffrey, that his friends called him 'Caff' and that his phone ringing throughout that hour was often as not one of his three adult children. His painting exhibitions in Shannon airport and Dublin airport of his images of James Joyce belied the fact that he'd spent his working life as a high flyer in the booze-distribution business before his wife died and he switched to painting.

'Joyce used to live here,' Caff said. 'There's a plaque outside on the wall. This place is mentioned in *Ulysses*.'

Our hour-long conversation eventually included a thirty-year-old newlywed recovering from cancer of the lymph glands who was also waiting for the CAT scan machine. The three of us couldn't have had a livelier conversation had we'd met at a fancy luncheon, and I was buzzing by the time it was my turn on the machine.

'I read *Joy* and loved it,' said the brown-haired, middle-aged nurse who instructed me to lie on my back.

My books had a life of their own. They were raising children who'd gone into the world alone and never called home, but sometimes strangers would mention that they'd sighted them. I was as excited to hear that Caff was writing a children's book as I was to discover that he'd begun painting after the trauma of losing his wife and the wrench of leaving a high-profile job. The way words live was about to bring love in my life in a way I couldn't have imagined. As it was, meeting Caff sent me buzzing back up to my room, where I apologised to Eamon and the waiting crew.

'But listen to what happened,' I said. 'It was so exciting. I just met this amazing guy while I was down having my CAT scan. Is there some way that we can include him in our filming? You know, let people see that a few hours spent in the X-ray department can be as exciting as a ho-down?'

What helped to explain my story was the large brown envelope that I'd found on my bed from Caff. The glossy photo images that he'd enclosed of four of his paintings included two of Joyce in Paris, and on the letter he'd written, he'd drawn a picture of me with hair, though of course I now had none.

But no, Eamon wasn't interested in including him in our

filming, though he let me stick the pictures of Caff's paintings on the wall behind my bed. There was no reason for Eamon to understand my reverence for serendipity. I sensed that someone had come into my life who would make a difference. How, why or when, I couldn't say. But I was sure of it, in the same way that I'd been sure a month earlier when I rang Delia Roche Kelly in St Vincent's Hospital and said that I would pop in to see her before I had my breast drained by my surgeon, Arnie Hill, who happened to be in the theatre there at the main hospital that morning.

When Delia and I first met, she brought out the ghetto in me. We were seated catacorner to each other at a ladies' dinner thrown by my friend, Clodagh Duff, at her house in Glenmacnass, near Glendalough, the spot once famed as a monks' retreat which now attracts tourists by the busload. That night I was recovering from flu, and Delia smoked her way through our four courses.

'White trash,' I said, shaking my head after leaving the table before the dessert because I was overcome by Delia's cigarette smoke. We'd not met before and I would have been pleased to never meet again, but she happened to get breast cancer and was in a room next to mine a month prior to my ten days at St Vincent's Private. It turned out to be another of those instances whereby cancer brings people together, because our breast cancer experience bound us like sisters.

During the late '80s, Delia had run a famous nightclub on Manhattan's Lower East Side before returning to her native Ireland to develop property she had in Greystones, about 15 miles from Dublin city centre. Building was in her blood, because she was born a Gallagher, her father and uncle being the noted Gallaghers, once infamous as the island's most prosperous men before Delia's brother Patrick contributed to the family's fame when he went bankrupt, not only losing their millions but also being jailed for losing some other people's as well.

All of this was very stale news by the morning in late December when I was driving myself to St Vincent's to see Arnie Hill and stopped at the store to pick up goodies for Delia, who was there in a four-bed ward.

'Aren't you paying the highest insurance band, Delia?' I asked when I sat on the edge of her bed. With the vomiting bug going around the hospital and me having caught MRSA in the private section, I figured she needed all the special care and privacy that a private room could offer.

'I like it here,' she said. 'But the food's terrible. My daughter will be bringing me something later.'

The thick waft of blonde hair she'd had at Clodagh Duff's dinner party was gone. Her baldness was almost hidden by a grey velvet hat. Her big pearl earrings and red fingernails belonged to ladies who shop. Though I still had all my hair, the fact that I knew it was going made me feel not an ounce of embarrassment about her baldness. Behind her glasses were the same big blue eyes that stared at me over the main course at dinner when I asked if she could kill the cigarettes.

We were both hard women, toughened by over half a century of experience, reinforced by public success and absolutely sure of ourselves. When breast cancer stuck us in a club together, placing us on the same fighting side, there was no time to play at being adversaries. We had to help keep each other alive. I was for Delia that morning when I brought a sandwich and yoghurt and sweets to the hospital.

And she was for me when she said, 'Don't you look fabulous?'

'I feel like shit. Drove here to get this wound drained. But why aren't you in a private room?'

Four weeks earlier, on 29 November when I'd checked into St Vincent's Private for my mastectomy, though Delia had been gone a month, she'd remained infamous with the hospital staff for the soirées in her private room. They loved relating how her long trail of visitors arrived in party spirit, some bringing exotic takeaway meals, others turning up with champagne or chocolates to ply Delia with the comforts to which she was accustomed. Finding her in a ward in the public hospital didn't feel right.

'Christmas holidays,' she said. 'They've closed so many wards to give the staff time off. They say that I'll get a private room as soon as one's available.'

'This is ridiculous, ' I said. 'Don't you pay top-dollar VHI insurance? And surely the one time that you need some molly-coddling is bloody Christmas time!'

At least she had a bed by the window, but as soon as somebody from the kitchen came and stood in the middle of the ward to reel off the day's dinner menu. I was irate for her again. Since Delia had had lumpectomies in both breasts as opposed to a mastectomy, she was feeling luckier than I was. But sitting there on the edge of her bed, I felt that both of us were unlucky to have had complications with our surgery. In my case it was the MRSA infection, in hers it was an infection in the area under her left arm where her lymph glands had been removed.

As intractable as she'd looked at Clodagh Duff's long dinner table exhaling smoke, Delia now struck me as being so vulnerable in a ward in a public hospital, despite how positive she was being. There she was in that bed, a woman in her 50s like me, trying to recover from breast cancer while complications placed her at added risk.

I didn't know then that her younger sister and their mother had died from breast cancer. I did know that Delia had a lot of fight in her, but I also knew that didn't mean that cancer wasn't going to take her out.

As I stood up, smoothing the cover that I'd wrinkled on her bed, I said, 'If I don't go back out and wait in reception, I might miss Arnie. Did you order dinner?'

'I can only eat the mashed potatoes. The only thing edible, darling . . .' she laughed.

It wasn't going to take long to discover that Delia had such a vivacious, indelible spirit that I was going to have to give her a street name.

'I'm callin' you Dee Dee,' I announced as soon as I got to know her better. She laughed and acquiesced. At the time, we were finishing a delicious lamb dinner that she'd cooked at her place in Greystones. She'd had it built from scratch. Like a developer's signature tune it was. Every inch gorgeous, from the two big bedrooms on the ground floor to the surprising living room above with the A-shaped wooden beams and open-plan kitchen at the far end.

Like Caff, Dee Dee has stories to tell that could keep you spellbound for a week. She can spiel tales about Delia's, her nightclub, dropping names of guests like Oprah Winfrey and Ted Kennedy, or relate her dealings with Lower East Side Puerto Ricans from the local protection racket that could have you laughing until tears fell. And like Caff, Dee Dee has that strong Irish family thing. You see her with her older brother, Danny, who has Down syndrome, and know that she, like Caff, has a heart for her family which knows no bounds. It all comes with that big, full-bodied laugh and a wild, crazy, unpredictable streak that makes both Caff and Dee Dee seem indomitable.

But are any of us?

Whenever I was with either of them, and it grew to be often, it was impossible not to wonder if we weren't on our way out.

*It is only with the heart that one can
see clearly: what is essential
is invisible to the eye.*

ANTOINE DE SAINT-ÉXUPERY

19

Slow Dancing in Cyberspace

As February was drawing to a close, friends kept saying, 'Don't you look amazing? You've got a glow!' They were still saying it in the spring, but what I didn't disclose until early summer is that I was in love. The circumstances were so bizarre that I'd decided that I'd keep them to myself. He and I had agreed that we mattered too much to each other to tell anyone else. What he didn't know is that I was breaking a promise to myself: 'No more secret affairs,' I'd said after what happened with Mick. But this was totally different. At least I thought it was. And keeping it secret made the love cut deeper and therefore sweeter.

This man's spirit was golden. His love for his dead wife was exhilarating. His love for his two daughters made me sit up and take notice. It was all so different from anything that I had known. Did men love women this much? I listened. And while listening and advising, while getting the most charming e-mails from a man I knew briefly when I was 18, I fell in love.

Try marrying the power of a secret to the potency of love. It's a dynamite concoction that pumps adrenalin through the bloodstream to provoke such a natural high that it's a cure-all like no other.

Loving Todd was so relevant to my response to chemo-therapy that if I don't mention it, you'll be cheated of info that explains why I didn't get the nausea or fatigue that mars chemotherapy's healing reputation. When everybody expected me to be a long-suffering chemo patient, I was whistling and singing and feeling so buzzed by love that I didn't need the pills prescribed to boost my energy and waylay nausea while I was getting Adriamycin, the toughest of the chemotherapy drugs intended to insure against a recurrence of breast cancer. In early April, I even sailed through a bout of pneumonia that landed me in hospital for a week. It felt no worse than a niggling cough, and when my oncologist, John McCaffrey, came to check on me, I asked, 'Think love might be a healer, since it increases your adrenalin, which gets your heart pumping double time?'

He didn't exactly agree but admitted that I wasn't reacting to chemo like most people. While I was in with pneumonia, though nurses would occasionally catch me dozing, because sitting in that hospital bed made me dozy, they also saw me exercising in my room each night and taking four flights of stairs rather than the hospital elevator.

I won't claim that I can explain how I came to be in love. I'm not sure I know myself, but I'll relate the circumstances, in which some personal history is involved. But whatever I tell you, what you mustn't forget is how much I wanted to stay alive.

When I left Berkeley and university in February of '66, I thought I was taking a term off to explore Europe. I had no idea that I wouldn't return or that I'd become locked into a foreign culture that distanced me from the person I'd been raised to be by my family and nation. American politics and its class system, better known as racism, had shaped and limited my life and future in ways that I couldn't know or fully comprehend until I was outside it. Being Negro had dominated my identity.

Growing up in the States, I was a Negro first and my individual Self second. We weren't yet called black and there was no Black Power. When I was in high school from 1960 to '64, and of dating age, Negroes and whites didn't date, but when I started as a freshman at the University of California in Berkeley, on our vast and liberal campus of 33,000 students, with about 120 of us being Negro, though social segregation was still the norm, a few daredevils like myself broke with tradition and crossed the colour bar. There was that element of tampering with the forbidden, so even holding hands in secret was pretty brave. With the arrival of the Pill came the freedom to sleep with boys. Though I only had one serious boyfriend in the 18 months that I was there, I had sex with a few others, one of whom was Mario Savio, who led the Free Speech Movement. Another was an architectural student named Todd. They weren't Negro, and America's entrenched racism was constantly in my face.

In contrast, when I arrived in London on 28 February 1966, my nationality became my identity, and the Negro label took a back seat. 'You're American,' people would say the minute I opened my mouth. There was such enormous passion for American culture at that time, from movies and music to art and fashion, that being from California was as much a plus as coming from the Berkeley campus, which had gained an international reputation as the hub of student protest through the Free Speech Movement.

Being 19, I adapted to London quickly, and it in turn embraced me. I lived each day to the full, like any young '60s adventure seeker, meeting new people and taking on new challenges as one day slid into the next and one hundred days became one thousand, one thousand became ten thousand. But who was counting? I was living. Forty years of layer upon layer of experience had broadened me. But despite work, travel and motherhood from London to Sydney, Munich to Milan, Paris to Dublin, still, at my centre, I was the girl from Berkeley.

Then one day in mid-February 2005, it was 17 February to be exact, that architectural student that I'd had a thing for when I was an 18-year-old Berkeley freshman turned up in my bedroom in the chalet that I was renting at the Bel Air. It was exactly 6.48 p.m. and dark out. While some light from a courtyard street lamp entered through a skylight, I lay wide awake but in bed, huddled under the duvet with only a small bedside lamp on. I was so cosy and warm that I resisted sitting up, because it was obvious from the sweat on the skylight that there was another grim winter's night ahead. As usual, on my little bedside table was my BlackBerry.

In case you've never handled a BlackBerry, envisage a flat and almost square mobile phone that's the size of a ten year old's hand. When a message comes through, it buzzes, and in the top left-hand corner of its two-inch-by-two-and-a-half-inch screen, a little icon appears to show that there's an e-mail. It can display about 40 words at a time but will receive or send a message of any length. But I didn't see the emotional importance of this until love came along.

I had grown dependent on e-mails to keep in touch with family and friends, and as so many of them lived in different time zones, I got used to receiving little e-mails all day and night: guided missiles of encouragement from people sending love and prayers. 'Thinking about you', 'Wishing you well', 'Lighting candles for you', 'Sending many kisses', 'Wish I could be there', 'Wish you were here' . . . The love and support was so constant that I knew that although I was entirely alone I was also sitting on the wings of many angels, many energies wanting me well. Having that little BlackBerry buzz with a message in the middle of the night, while Ireland slept, suited my needs and my peculiar sleep habits. In the dead of night, while I lay in bed thinking, suddenly the silence would be broken by that little buzz, and somebody's few words would boost me.

Maybe it would be 4.30 a.m. and it would be a cryptic few words from Karis, 'Here with Dono thinking of u', Dono being Donovan Leitch Junior, only son of the singer Donovan and Enid, or maybe at midnight it would be my friend Bassam just saying, 'Love you, Missy', or maybe as the sheep in the Bel Air's meadow behind me bleated, a long message would sail in from Deborah in Santa Fe, who called me her bosom buddy, because she was in recovery from a mastectomy, too.

During the wee hours of 16 February, it was dark out and dim in my bedroom when an e-mail came from my old Berkeley friend, Andrea Luria, who was living in LA and had come to my hair-cutting party. Her e-mail had me frustrated, because there was an attachment with her text, and I hadn't yet learned how to open attachments. Early the following morning, a Wednesday, when I was attempting to open it again, I noticed the list of other recipients. One name was that of the architectural student whom I'd slept with in Berkeley in '65, when crossing the colour bar was not the done thing – which, he said, his Polish mother had reminded him of in Yiddish after he'd introduced us.

Forty years on, seeing his name stirred my curiosity. At 7.30 a.m., as I was tapping out his e-mail address on my BlackBerry, I had no sense that I was doing something that would save my life. What's notable with hindsight is how quick and easy it was to type seven words and press SEND.

'I'm Marsha Hunt, are you Todd Mendelson?'

'I am. are you marshah from berkeley?' was his answer six hours later. No capitals and my name spelled wrong. But his sudden 'presence' was mind-boggling.

After 40 years, I was in Ireland and where was he? It could've been anywhere from Johannesburg to Waikiki, Hong Kong or Maine. Though it was early evening, I was tucked up in bed, because I'd decided naps were crucial to my recovery, not only from the mastectomy but also the MRSA and the intravenous antibiotics that had taken a heavy toll on my body. Alone and silent with no one to confer with, a small miracle had happened.

After 40 years, the fact that he didn't physically materialise made it all the more extraordinary to suddenly be in touch with this boy that I had touched and let touch me back in the days when I was still called a Negro and was meant to be off limits for him. Was he still brave? Did he still dare to break away from the pack?

I could recall his profile, neck and jawline and pretty lips, but at the same time I expected that he'd aged like other Berkeley friends who'd been at the hair-cutting party. Was he fat or thin, grey or bald, homely or as handsome as he'd once been?

As I stared at Todd's brief message like it was hieroglyphics, instead of a multitude of questions about him tumbling through my mind, I was dumbstruck. Shocked. Awed. And maybe even a touch frightened . . . This small BlackBerry in my palm suddenly awakened me to a terrifying fact: for us humans, distance and time had ceased to be what they had been. They were now outmoded concepts. If everybody with an e-mail address was as easy to track down, then the joys of privacy and anonymity had seen their day. If so, then this little magical message bearer is as good as the CIA!

How soon would its negatives outweigh its positives? For the moment, I was glad that it had let my past catch up with my present. Berkeley 1965 was in Ireland 2005.

My year had begun with so many pluses: Kathy's 5,000-euro cheque, Stuart Prebble filming my Lichfield session, my clean bill of health from MRSA, five sunny days in LA, and the hair-cutting party with all the joys of seeing family and friends and playing granny to Mazie and baby Zach. With my single-breasted bald image, 17 days into chemotherapy, I was moving right along, defying predictions that I'd be sick. Instead, on that cold February day, I was high on life when my seven words and his journeyed through cyberspace, which I then imagined as a brilliant sunset meeting the horizon. But is cyberspace not space at all but merely thoughts transferred in the time it takes to write a message, address it and press SEND?

Of course, there remains the deeper mystery of why I chose to e-mail Todd at all, and why he bothered to respond, and why I bothered to write again. In answer to his, 'I am. are you marshah from berkeley?' I wrote back, 'Yep. And I'm in

Dublin, about 6,000 miles from Berkeley. And 40 years. How's by you and where are you?'

What was unexpected was that eight weeks earlier, his wife of 37 years had died of cancer. My heart bled for him and their two adult daughters. And a secret I harbour stepped in: I've been told that I'm a healer, and hearing of his emotional pain, I wanted to heal him. This has got me in trouble before and was about to get me in trouble again.

By the time that our first day of e-mailing, Thursday, 17 February, was drawing to a close, the info we'd exchanged was pretty nebulous. I knew that he was in Virginia and planning a trip to Italy in the spring. And among the things I wrote before turning in was:

> I'm having chemotherapy as a post boob cancer treatment. Right boob gone. Don't miss it. Wasn't doing much with it, and cancer has been pretty good. Lots of flowers, presents, bonding and discoveries. Even a great job came with it. Because English TV is doing an hour documentary about my cancer. Did I last see you in '65? I've lived in Europe since '66, but inasmuch as my family lived in the Bay Area, I made frequent trips to Berkeley. Karis is London born and raised but went to Yale and then moved to California. I'll be in and out of France in May. Chemo will keep me popping in and out of Dublin too. I used to visit Milan a lot but don't know the rest of Italy. The world is soooo big, sooo various, soooo splendid.
>
> Hope Emeryville has been good to you.
> Love,
> Marsha from Berkeley

That was Thursday. By Saturday our e-mails were boomeranging back and forth. I was almost sorry that one included his photo, because, as he said himself, at nearly 65, he was no longer the smooth-faced boy I'd last seen at Berkeley. Still, his craggy face had a certain elegance, enhanced by the sadness in his eyes, which said more than his comical e-mails. He could have me laughing until the tears rolled, and the combination of his humour and his love for his deceased wife and their two adult daughters warmed me to him as much as discovering that he employed a mutual friend from our college days.

Having never had a long-term partner, I could only use my skill as a novelist to imagine the indescribable vacuum created by the loss of a loving wife. Since '68 when I was in *Hair*, which seemed too long ago to remember, they'd shared life.

If being heard can ease emotional pain, Todd had found an e-mail 'listener', who knew cancer from both his and his wife's perspective. I knew things that he dared not voice and things she could no longer voice. And it was added good fortune that his daughters being almost my daughter's age helped me to understand a bit about them, too.

After nine days, we knew so much about one another and our communications were so deeply charged and very special that I refused to erase any of them. One I sent from my laptop said:

> Women like me are a dime a dozen. Sniffing at your coat tail and making eyes at you. Be fooled by none of us.
>
> Let your infatuation be with life and stumbling upon a mate will happen. You may be too much in

215

pain for one right now, and it's possible that I've happened along a bit too soon for you to meet me halfway.

And while it may be that you need to close the shutters on your life, cancer has thrown mine open. I'm ready to fall in love for the first time in years. That's a fact and these e-mails between us bare that fact for me.

Here I am a bit giddy at the sight of your name and yet you're naturally still very much in mourning and surrounded by stop signs. Yield signs.

I accepted that he was unable to speak on the phone and that e-mails would be our sole form of communication. By this means, he said, he told me things that he'd not even told his wife. In turn, I sometimes told him what I dared not admit to myself, let alone repeat to someone else. He said that we were like two kids hiding in the bushes, holding hands while telling secrets. I said we were flickering candles to guide us to another place.

He wrote tenderness into each line about his wife. Reading him was a warm fire to ease the chill of Ashford's winter's night. Each letter was another puff of helium, filling my spirit and lifting me higher. I wanted no explanation for what we were doing or why. He was my balm. I was his.

On day ten of our communication, I had to spend the afternoon getting chemotherapy treatment. With an overhead drip draining into my vein, while I sat up, tapping out a letter to him on my BlackBerry, I wasn't alone, I was with him.

I hadn't been with a man for years. Not since Alan. Nor had I been looking for one. Somehow Jimi had filled that space. I'd been single-minded and passionate about understanding and registering his unique place in social history. My solitary writing life suited me, with my independence letting me be where necessary to research him. But cancer had placed Jimi on a back seat, and before I had a chance to restore him to a front one, there was a living, breathing broken man in the palm of my hand night and day.

Imagine that it's the cold of an Irish winter's night. I'm alone in the car, both hands on the wheel, heading back to the chalet. It's raining. No music plays, so the sound of the windscreen wipers is all the more noticeable. When the BlackBerry beeps, I know instinctively that it'll be Todd's name on the little screen. I pull in at a service station, turn on the light and see that he has written, 'Sleep with me as I with you, soft as a pussy willow. Let me share your warmth, your love and take from me. Thank you.'

With just the faintest recollection of our daring time in each other's arms in '65, what I'd forgotten is that he was as unconventional as I was. What I hadn't forgotten was his handsome face and his erect cock. It was circumcised and as fine as any sculpture. I can still see it. And one April afternoon, while I was walking across the bridge in central Dublin near Memorial Road, Todd's tanned young face came to mind. As I tingled all over, his cock flashed next. I was unable to contain my laughter as I passed people. I looked so respectable, dressed to the nines, but there I was, striding along while envisioning a cock that I hadn't seen for 40 years. Yet, at that moment, it was so clear in my mind that I could have painted the shape, the colour, the beautiful head. 'You're a disgrace!' I chided myself, giggling and enjoying the breeze and sun and the memory of Todd's glorious member.

That evening, when I wrote him about this episode, I

knew that he wouldn't be the least bit embarrassed or think me odd. Nothing I said seemed to surprise him, and he could give as good as he got.

After he e-mailed me a shot taken of him with a business partner in Hawaii, I carried it in my wallet, and he said he'd do the same if I sent one of me. What was nice was that he specifically asked for a bald one. I never asked if he actually carried it around, but I did his and would take it out in the damnedest places, like a church or while I was hooked up for a chemo fix. Seeing him looking bronzed in the Hawaiian sun always empowered my spirit. I assume that's what love is, when just seeing a photo of somebody that you 'talk' to every day strengthens your resolve and makes it easy to take on whatever's next.

Our e-mails flew back and forth fast and furious, with a temporary pause when he had to go to Asia and was going to be moving around so fast that he opted out of staying in touch. By then, I was addicted to his letters, addicted to his confidences, addicted to the hope that in the near future we would touch again. While he was gone, I got a lot of joy out of sending him things: handwritten letters, a favourite framed picture of a younger me with Karis, snaps of la montagne . . . I was so crazy in love that I even sent him the key. Being in love had me so high I would have walked barefoot on glass to reach him, and the chemotherapy wasn't affecting me at all.

I loved going for my chemo sessions and being able to answer no to the checklist of possible suffering.

Nope. Not nauseaous.

Nope. Not a bit tired.

Nope. No mouth ulcers.

No. No headaches.

No. No constipation and no diarrhoea.

Appetite? Great.

Nope. No dodgy libido. In fact, libido pumping . . .

When I e'd Todd describing a Wicklow snowstorm that I was seeing at that moment or he e'd me describing the thunder and lightning of a rain storm in Virginia, I was in his head, he was in mine – all the while sharing secrets and jokes or delving into some of life's pleasures and delusions. We stayed current and rarely spoke of our past, but for certain we were also bound by a memory of each other as daring students making love on a Berkeley veranda in a bright north-side apartment that I shared with two other girls. 'Are you still so soft?' he once asked. I didn't know. No one had ever intimated that I was especially soft, so I didn't know what to answer.

I knew he was suffering badly from the loss of his wife. Her death left in him a void that he wasn't ready to fill. Yet I was sure that the crazy things I wrote and sent penetrated his sadness, rained laughter upon him, gave him a moment's joy and made him feel adored, despite his overwhelming loneliness. And, oh, the childish pleasure I got from trying to give him pleasure and let him know that someone heard, someone was listening, so I was forever answering his e-mails.

One he sent about his sense of loss was such poetry that I typed it in big letters and pinned it on my wall. Writing to him with news of my day or thoughts about his was a hit of helium to lift me above the clouds. Did I feel sick? Not a bit!

My concern was that if like his wife I had terminal cancer, Todd would have to endure another lingering cancer death, so although I pushed to meet, it was also a relief that he restricted our contact to e-mailing, which eventually included the odd phone call, when I'd blush like a child and admit to being shy.

When he'd buzz on my BlackBerry, whether it was by my bedside or in my handbag, I'd pause to write back instantly, and if my e-mail flashed while he was working on his office computer in Virginia, and he responded immediately, what was the distance between his thoughts and mine?

Ten days after we 'met', those 3,000 miles between us dissolved as I drove to Belfast in late February and kept stopping to retrieve his mail and send mine. Whenever I recall that journey, I shall always remember Todd being with me. Because he was.

And that March night when I sat parked in the rain, teeming it was, outside a brick basilica in northern France, having just retrieved his e-mail, I dared not leave the spot until I'd sent words whizzing back. And the time his e-mail buzzed my BlackBerry while I sat in a London taxi as it rounded past Buckingham Palace, I e'd straight back to describe where we were. There he was in Virginia before the business day started, yet he was also in London with me as I wrote back describing the gorgeous cherry blossoms and the hordes of tourists that 'we' drove past.

I love writing. Word play is as essential to my being as singing with a band once was. I use them to paint images and clarify my thoughts, so I had an unfair advantage, because before I came along, Todd said he didn't write. But we wrote hundreds of pages between us, and while it was a diary of his sadness, it was also a record of his reawakening and sometimes an embarrassing declaration of my love for this broken man.

'What does it matter if he loves you?' said my homoeopath,

Marie Doyle. We were having tea at the Merrion Hotel. Since Alan's cancer, she'd invested so much of her time and love in keeping me mentally and physically well that it seemed deceitful not to explain why I glowed.

'Am I wasting my time on a bereaved widower?' I asked.

'What matters is that loving him makes you feel wonderful. So why give that up?'

Until that moment I'd imagined that being in love required both parties. The notion that it could work just as well for one nearly had me dancing on the ceiling.

'You mean he doesn't have to love me for me to get a thrill out of loving him?'

'Course not. Loving him is making you well. Look at you! You positively shine. Who'd ever believe that you're in the middle of having chemo?'

I hadn't really considered the health aspects of letting go of my feelings.

I want to live.

Was being in love keeping me well?

How does love affect the human body?

What are its medicinal qualities?

If being in love lifts the spirit and empowers the psyche, does it cure on other levels?

After leaving Mary, I e-mailed myself from my laptop to my BlackBerry, and it's a message I'd check from time to time whenever I began to ask myself if I was wasting my time with Todd. It says, 'Being in love makes me happy. It makes me wake up singing. It makes me kinder, more tolerant of others.' Then I threw in that line that he once wrote that his wife told their daughter. She said, 'Love makes the heart strong.'

Practically every time I'd tell some close friend confidentially that I was in love and would reveal that I hadn't seen my heartthrob for 40 years and didn't know if I'd see him again, the question each one asked was if Mr Cyberspace, as I referred to him, was in love with me.

'Does it matter?' I'd say, using Mary Doyle's line. 'What matters is that I love him.'

'It's just a fantasy. You'll get over it,' a couple of them said. I didn't say that I didn't want to get over it, because it felt good and feeling good was vital, and possibly reviving cells that were being battered by chemotherapy. It harmed no one. It cost nothing. And Todd said not only did I bring him joy, I also gave him some of life's answers.

'I don't have to cook or pick up his socks,' I told one friend, to which she replied, 'And nor do you have to fight over who's going to sleep on the wet patch.'

The wet patch?

I hadn't had sex in so long that I'd forgotten there *was* a wet patch . . .

My idea of romancing in cyberspace is more innocent than out-and-out sex. It's more like slow dancing. Like that one we used to do when I was 13 and still living in Philly. It was called the Grind, and I'm amazed that it ever went out of style, because although it was kind of low down, it passed muster with the parents.

Imagine a girl and boy, dressed to party, in a cheek-to-cheek embrace. Her left arm is around his neck, her right hand is in his left, which he presses back against her shoulder, while his other arm holds her so tightly that all you can slide between them is sweat. Locked at the hip, they barely move enough with the beat to call it dancing.

When Todd sent an e-mail to say he was taking up ballroom dancing, I thought it was a joke, But the next thing I knew he was describing how some little Southern belle was teaching him to rumba, I laughed, before I cried.

'Sugar,' I wrote back, 'I can teach you to dance.'

But it wasn't the rumba I had in mind. My secret desire was to teach him the Grind.

*Don't give up, your miracle
is on the way.*

20

Stepping Out

It wasn't in my nature to be passive about something as radical as the certain change in my appearance imposed by cancer and chemotherapy. As soon as I was told I would lose my right breast and then suffer a temporary weight gain and hair loss due to chemotherapy, I knew it was essential to come up with a look that suited my age and the change in my hair and body shape. Having refused plastic surgery to create a fake breast, being single breasted was going to be permanent, but being bald and overweight would only last for eight to ten months. Since nothing could prevent it, it was common sense to relax and enjoy the experience.

It seemed obvious that without hair, hats and earrings would become a crucial part of my wardrobe, and those beautiful nineteenth-century earrings from Mick came into their own. What surprised me is how many women knew they were diamonds, since I wouldn't know diamonds from diamante. Nurses at the hospital, doctors, lawyers, waitresses, several of my girlfriends – they all seemed to have an eye which I lacked, and it boosted my ego to hear, 'What gorgeous earrings' or 'Love the earrings' or 'You wouldn't like to give me just one of those?'

I needed all the compliments, because even on good days I thought I looked like the bald rapper Tupac Shakur, while on bad days I thought I resembled the bald heavyweight George Foreman, a good deal older than he'd been as the world champion. It was just as well that some friends said they preferred me bald, because after a month of chemotherapy, I grew balder. Despite the close shave I got at the hair-cutting party on 25 January, a month later I was waking each day to find my pillow covered in black specks. My short hair was coming out at the root. It was hideous the way it clung to the pillowcase, and I knew those specks would have been clumps of long hair had I not already had my head shaved.

The back of my head was first to become totally hairless. It was as smooth as a baby's bottom. Then I noticed that my eyebrows were gradually thinning, but not only didn't I mind, they looked more modern and I wondered why I hadn't plucked them sooner.

My body was a different story. The flesh around the site of my operation was contorted by the combination of the welts caused by the strips and the MRSA infection. It looked as though it had been burned as well as cut, and a surgeon friend I showed it to shook his head and said, 'That will need plastic surgery.' Yet it bothered me less than my weight gain from steroids, which are given intravenously before chemo as part of the therapy.

However much I beamed due to the secret e-mails from Todd, and however much anyone said, 'Don't you look well!', the mirror told me to make the maximum effort whenever I stepped out of the house. It was no time for half measures, because how well I looked determined how well people imagined I felt. And how well they imagined I felt made them less likely to whisper among themselves that I was dying. If I was dying, so be it, but I considered it negative to have people burying me before I was in my grave.

As I had declared at the time it was given to me at St Vincent's Private, the false breast with bra never got worn. It was a matter of pride. Why pretend I had a breast when I didn't? I saw no shame in being single breasted, but it did mean that I had to rethink my wardrobe. I decided that it would take some daring to wear the form-fitting cashmere sweater with the deep V neck which I'd received at Christmas. The same was true of a couple of dresses. Ready-to-wear clothes are designed for two breasts, so with my single breast, almost every top and dress I owned looked ill fitting.

What I'd better reiterate here is that I had limited funds. Had I been flush, it would've been easy enough to rush out and buy a new wardrobe. My situation required some luck, some cunning and some imagination.

On the luck side, my friend, Consolata Boyle, designs clothes for films, but having just won an Emmy for her designs for HBO's *The Lion In Winter*, starring Glenn Close, I figured Consolata was very much in demand and the most I could ask for was advice. At the time – this was prior to me getting MRSA – I needed a dress for Tim Curry's opening night in Chicago in mid-January. Consolata, being the woman she is, not only turned up in my hospital room but arrived with yards of the most beautiful fabric, a heavy, burnt orange silk. Now all I needed was a dressmaker, and of all the people I asked, including the nurses, it was Clodagh Duff's partner, Ib Jorgensen, himself once a couturier, who helped. He rang Thomas Wolfangel, the tailor and dressmaker who used to work with Ib.

To have Consolata and Thomas meet in my hospital room was rejuvenating. Hearing the soft-spoken Consolata toss dress-making terms like 'cut on the bias' and 'ballerina length' about while Thomas took my measurements made me feel that my body was a challenge being addressed by artists. It was fabulous and so much of what I thought being single breasted should be about: the chance to be creative and inspire Amazon fashions. High fashion dares to be bold and exciting. Some of the high-end shows are like art in motion: skinny young models used like hangers prance out to display what no woman would dare wear in the street.

'I'll have special one-tit bras made,' I joked when Thomas said that the bra I wore would be so important for the dress which he was about to rush off and make for me. But MRSA meant that the first night I'd planned to attend took place without me, and the long wraparound dress that Consolata designed and Thomas made hung like an abandoned dream in my bedroom closet at the chalet.

In mid-February, when I heard that Paul Nicholas was opening in Belfast in a musical *Dr Jekyll and Mr Hyde*, which he was also producing, the fact that it was going to take place on the 28th, which was the 39th anniversary of my arrival in Britain, made it seem fated that I should go. When Stuart Prebble and Eamon O'Connor included it in the shooting schedule for the documentary, the date went into my diary as a definite.

When we were in the London production of *Hair*, Paul was my boyfriend. Although our relationship ended after six months, because I left to become a Track Records artist, we remained good friends and I came to know and adore his powerful father, Oscar Beuselinck, who was the solicitor for some of the biggest names in show business in Britain before he died in 1998. Before Paul became best known for his role in the TV sitcom *Just Good Friends*, his career in musicals included the lead in *Hair*, *Jesus Christ Superstar*, *Grease* and *Cats*. Despite all his talent, glory and good looks, what's most likeable about him is that he's shy and has a wicked sense of humour. Any time we're together, we laugh more than we talk. In Belfast, it was no different.

I sat in the dress circle watching him rehearse for that evening's first-night performance. Despite being a floor above and a hundred feet from the stage, he managed to throw me a line that had me screaming with laughter. I was also laughing in his dressing-room while the camera for my cancer documentary was rolling. The make-up lady was adjusting Paul's jet-black wig for his role as Dr Jekyll. As she pulled it down over his blond hair, I asked him what he thought of my bald head.

Now, we've known each other for 37 years, I know his wife, Linzi, and have met their kids and his kids from his previous marriage. That's to say, I know Paul well and, since he's not a big talker, I can often gauge what he's thinking better from his eyes than the words that come out of his mouth. When I asked about my bald look, he said, 'I think your hair looks great, Marsh,' but he had paused a little too long and looked a little too earnest.

'What?' I said. 'You hate it!'

'What do you mean?' he said, trying not to laugh.

'I can tell by your eyes, Paulie!'

'I think you look good,' he said straight-faced, still holding back a laugh.

'You're a lying bastard!' I said and we fell about laughing, although nobody else crammed into his dressing-room found our exchange as funny as we did. He was looking in the mirror and couldn't stop laughing. Nor could I, which made filming so difficult that the camera stopped rolling.

Paul's not the only one from *Hair* that I'm still close to. There's Sheila Scott Wilkinson, who's still one of my closest friends, as is Tim Curry, who wasn't in the cast for our rehearsals but replaced somebody when we were a couple of months into the show.

Although I was only in the show for six months, I rarely see my name in print without *Hair* being mentioned. It's odd being part of a myth that I know bears no relation to the truth. Paul was the star of that show, he and Oliver Tobias, and the only reason I ran away with so much publicity was my big afro, which was then a political statement about being black. After *Hair*'s first night in London, I was photographed by fashion photographers like Lichfield and David Bailey, which turned that political statement into a fashion statement. Thirty-seven years on, the absence of my hair, my baldness, was again a political statement. Cancer is becoming the plague of my generation. Why hide it? If enough of us come out bald and single breasted or breastless, more questions will be asked and more answers demanded about the breast cancer blight.

It was my first big night out with my bald head. Wearing a fur-collared jacket made by Thomas Wolfangel. I was a bit over dressed for the theatre in Belfast, but I'd had fun in my room at the Europa Hotel getting ready to go out and loved having two female ushers at the theatre stop me to say that my bald head looked great.

When I thanked them, I said, 'You really like it? This is my chemo look.'

They eyed each other. 'Really?'

They looked alike, so I wasn't that surprised to hear that

they were sisters. 'I wish our sister was here,' they said. 'She's had breast cancer.'

I was getting used to this. It seemed as though everybody I talked to knew someone or was related to somebody with breast cancer. My question is how come? Why are there so many with this disease and will the numbers continue to escalate?

Who's next?

Your sister?

Your mother?

Your grandmother?

Your girlfriend?

Or you?

We are all in the gutter. But some of us are looking at the stars.

OSCAR WILDE

21

Finding Jimi

Patient patient.

They look like the same word and sound alike? True, but in my case the first was an adjective and the second a noun. The noun is someone getting medical treatment, and the adjective means various things. One is the ability to endure waiting or delay. Another is the ability to tolerate being hurt, provoked, or annoyed without complaining or blowing one's top, and it can also mean to calmly persevere.

I'd been a patient patient since that Tuesday morning, 30 November, when Mr Arnie Hill and his surgical team amputated my right breast. But on the first of March, after seeing Paulie's musical and celebrating the 39th anniversary of my arrival in London, I woke at the Europa Hotel and didn't want to be the patient patient any longer. I wanted out of the noun. I wanted to get shod of the adjective. I wanted to be my healthy impatient self again, the person who got out of bed and, without so much as brushing her teeth or drinking a glass of water, hit the outdoors and walked for an hour. I wanted to be surer of my body than anybody living. I wanted my freedom. And the feeling grew even stronger after I got in my VW and headed out of Belfast.

It had been an extraordinary morning, not least because I'd been in a meeting with Eamon O'Connor about what we'd shot the night before, and so I hadn't been checking my BlackBerry. It was noon before I noticed that Todd had e'd me three times in response to me writing him in the middle of the night to say that something he'd written had hurt me deeply. It was nearly 1 p.m. when I'd piled my bag and laptop into my car in the hotel's drive. I was about to pull off before I suddenly remembered to switch on my BlackBerry. Seeing that I had three Todd messages was a first, because we'd established the habit of answering each other quickly. That I hadn't responded to his first message would have seemed odd enough to him, and odder still that I hadn't responded an hour later to his second. So with hindsight, I can see why he'd grown impatient for a response by his third message, but how he expressed this was by e-mailing, 'Goddammit answer me, I'm in pain.'

Now, while him saying that he was in pain should have instantly made me feel sympathetic, the statement made me burst out laughing. I couldn't budge from the spot, while I reread those six words and guffawed some more, before regaining enough composure to respond. Having not been in my presence in 40 years, this man hadn't got the measure of me.

It would be an overstatement to say I'm tough, but however anyone would describe me, under no circumstances does my demeanour suggest that I'm the sort of woman that would take being ordered about. Any man I'm seeing innately understands this, so I was astonished to see the words 'Goddammit answer me'. Rather than anger me, however, it gave me the giggles. And to read that my hurt could cause him pain was such a revelation that it too lifted the natural guard of this patient patient who leapt out of bed that morning ready not only for a new day but a new beginning.

Perhaps being in Northern Ireland had more to do with it than I realised. Seeing Queen Elizabeth on a stamp I bought at the hotel reception to send a postcard, seeing my bill in pounds and pence instead of euros, dropping the card into a red mailbox common to Britain as opposed to one of Ireland's green ones, all of it was a reminder that although I had not left the island, I was travelling again. I'd left the safety of Ireland, my cancer base, and braved another country in which I had no medical affiliation and I'd managed. Didn't that prove that I was ready to go further afield?

I was in a precarious situation. I was a writer who was writing e-mails as opposed to books. I was a patient patient, and unless I did something radical, I was in danger of being so distanced from the project for which I'd risked my health and my life that the project itself was now at risk. It was imperative that I find Jimi. And for me, he was alive nowhere in Ireland, since Noel Redding's death two years earlier. Did I dare head back to France?

My four desks at la montagne bore proof of my enduring dedication to complete a book that wasn't a book until the last word was written. Bits of dated paper, a full sheet here, a scrap there, discarded drafts, files bulging with four years of research, receipts going back to 2000 that in themselves were reminders of where I'd been in search of James Marshall Hendrix: my working life was registered in all that. Yet my life itself depended upon restoring my health, and the truth is that cancer had not weakened my resolve but ridding my body of the cancerous tumour and the lymph glands under my right arm had radically reduced my strength. I tired easily. There were times when staying awake in the afternoon was a test. There were times when it felt like a horse had kicked me in the chest. There were times when I needed help but had none. Yet the way forward was to admit none of this, neither to myself nor anyone else. It was time to be strong and reclaim Jimi, dead thirty-four years, yet alive in me for five.

Living in my head comes easily. It's a professional necessity. What are to others no more than vain imaginings, wasted daydreams, fleeting thoughts, these are for me the lifeblood of my occupation. My three novels set in three different eras and littered with characters depended upon letting my imagination sprinkle upon blank pages until they mounted up and were published as books. But to get to that final stage takes resilience and mine was being consumed by my health, by me being the patient patient. I was revving up to be in a hurry . . .

Two weeks after Belfast, it was Todd's scheduled trip to India and Pakistan that gave me the bottle to pop into the Bel Air's reception and announce to Fidelma, 'With luck, I should be out of Number 3 by tomorrow night.'

Who was I kidding? It was the middle of March. Though I'd been renting the chalet since November, it looked like I had been there for years. The walls were lined with my pictures, the drawers were being used as files for bills, correspondence and art supplies for making cards. Winter coats filled one closet. Clothes filled another, and the vestiges of having been in hospital, first with cancer of breast and lymphs, then with MRSA, occupied a lot of space. Antiseptics and bandages, syringes and pill bottles, bed pads and heating pads, homoeopathic medicines – there was an eclectic assortment of items, including those for hair care, which stretched across those four months between my arriving with cancer yet feeling well, to my returning ill from hospital, followed by three months of gradual recovery to that stage whereby I believed that I was strong enough to drive to France.

Wanting to leave the three-bedroom chalet looking as immaculate as it had when I moved in was a tall order to set for myself, and with three days of intense effort, I nearly managed. But when I rang Fidelma from Dublin Port, just as I was about to drive onto the ferry, I said, 'Had I cleaned the stairs, I would have missed this boat.'

'Not to worry, Marsha,' she said. With her husband, Bill, dead only three months, Fidelma managed to be as hard working and understanding as ever.

It was 17 March, St Patrick's Day, a national holiday in Ireland in honour of its patron saint and an auspicious day for me to be setting out on an ambitious solo journey that would include the drive from the ferry port at Holyhead in Wales to the British Midlands and on south to Dover on the coast, where I expected to catch another car ferry to Calais, which is 70 miles north-west of my writing studio.

When I rose at 4 a.m. that morning, I never imagined that I would not see la montagne until nearly 3 a.m. the following day, and though I disclaimed accusations that the journey was too much for me while undergoing chemotherapy, the proof is that three weeks later, I was in the Mater Private Hospital with pneumonia.

But pneumonia is not cancer, and not only had I ceased to be the patient patient, I'd found a bit of Jimi there among the cobwebs. It wasn't just the pictures of him on my desk in the living room, or the pages about him that I'd been working on before I closed the house on 15 October to fly to New York, I had studied his life in there. I had walked the long hill talking to him. I had promised him that I would cast his life in new light. And now here I was, a little bent with pain but not bowed.

Be not forgetful to entertain strangers,
for thereby some have entertained
angels unawares.

EPISTLE OF PAUL TO THE HEBREWS 13:2

22

May Day

Exactly two months after that St Patrick's Day trip to la montagne, I was overjoyed to find myself there again. The late tulips were in full bloom. Some were fire-engine red, others a screaming yellow, and their heads were so fat that their stems were bending with the weight. Under the big pine, the maroon peonies were equally outstanding and overshadowed the nearby rows of lilies of the valley which were growing so wild that they were pushing up through the cement on the drive beside the garage. Every time there was the slightest breeze, their sweet scent wafted down the lane where I stood opening the mailbox and trying to guess who the two personal letters were from before checking the addresses.

Everywhere in the village was a heavenly green, and la montagne was looking her best. I'd been cutting the lawns and cutting back the shrubs and trees with the passion of someone proving a point: my right arm, weakened by surgery, was not going to turn my few acres into a jungle. I refused to let my new physical limitations restrict me . . . I will, I can, I fucking can,

I bloody will . . .When the strength wasn't in my right arm, it had been in my swearing, in my goading myself to do more.

Now, at the mailbox, with the day's delivery in my hand, I was proud of my work and prouder still of my garden. Not that anyone with a green thumb would give it a second look. They would notice the weeds growing up through the grate outside the front gate and probably wonder why everything wasn't cut back more. Having been in hospital with pneumonia the previous month, however, I now knew that overdoing it would land me back in trouble and was pleased with what I had managed to achieve.

I instantly recognised the handwriting on both the personal letters in my hand as I headed back to the house. Steve Lovi so frequently sends cards from San Francisco that his handwriting is as familiar to me as my own, and though I rarely get mail any more from Sonia Lane, back when she was typing my manuscripts, it wasn't unusual to get post from her a few times a week. Her precise print reminded me of being in elementary school, when so much importance was placed on neatness. And it was that quality which pleased me so much when I would send her sloppy pages that she would type so beautifully on her electric typewriter that my work looked like it had come from a laser printer before there was such a thing.

Before I opened her letter, I went indoors and sat at the table in the conservatory. It was obvious that she'd sent more than a letter and as I tore into the envelope, I could see that it was a newspaper clipping. Noel Redding's face was in the fold, which immediately put me off reading the article. Nonetheless, I scanned the caption under his photograph.

I hate reading about people I know. Journalists are normally off the mark. In this case, it was a Folkestone publication, which made the likelihood of it getting Noel wrong all the higher. He'd grown up there and for nine years, from '86 until '95, Folkestone had been my main base. This coincidence became a major bond between Noel and I, because who in the rock business knew Folkestone? Now, there I sat with the article about Noel in my hands. He'd been dead for two years and six days, and I felt badly that I'd forgotten to ring Deborah on the anniversary of his death.

I knew that her health had been declining, and it had been a couple of weeks since I'd rung. She was still staying with her sister, Alexis, in Santa Fe. In February, I'd encouraged her to sell the house in West Cork to raise some cash for herself, and though I went to a good deal of trouble to get two property developers whom I trusted to look at the Ardfield property, their quotes being much lower than Deborah may have expected didn't please her. It seemed to distance her from me, and I realised that she might have questioned my integrity. From my point of view, I knew how much time and effort I'd devoted to helping her when I wasn't well myself, but I had subsequently been e-mailing her less.

The Folkestone article was just the nudge that I needed to remind me that life was short. Grabbing the keys to the car and my BlackBerry, I went to send her sister a message. Reception at la montagne was poor, and though I could sometimes receive messages, sending them meant driving to a village five miles away, and on bad days even further.

I'd last seen Deborah when I'd made a visit ten months earlier to the house in West Cork. I'd been threatening to drive down to see her since she'd moved back to Ireland, and I was a couple of hours away visiting another friend when I decided that I'd take advantage of being halfway there. When she didn't answer her phone, I rang our mutual friend, June, who lives nearby. June assured me that Deborah was around and would love to see me, but the house was shut and she was nowhere in sight when I looked around. After waiting for half an hour, I was about to leave her a note when, in my rear-view mirror, I spotted a woman approaching. She was so thin, I didn't realise that it was Deborah until she was peering at me through the passenger window.

I said, 'I just rang June to ask where you might be.'

'Oh, shit,' said Deborah. 'I don't believe it. You've outed me!'

She'd spent the night at a hospital in Cork and didn't want anyone to know. It was during that hospital stay that she discovered that her cancer had moved to her second breast.

Deborah, who was 50, was beautiful. But that afternoon, she looked wan, and after heating the soup I'd brought, and insisting that she go to bed after she'd eaten, I advised her that the legal hassles over the house weren't good for her health.

With hindsight, thinking back to that afternoon visit, what's odd is that unbeknownst to me, I had cancer myself.

It was around 10 p.m. that 17 May when I got a response from Deborah's sister to the e-mail which I'd sent earlier, asking how Deborah was doing. It was such a beautifully worded e-mail that Alexis and Nancy, Deborah's other sister, sent to a list of Deborah's friends saying that she'd been brave until the end, and holding both their hands, she had died that morning.

Though it was the middle of May, it was chilly out, so I had a big log fire burning. With my BlackBerry still in my hand, I headed for the kitchen, noting how strange it was that despite the poor reception at la montagne, this message from Santa Fe had managed to come through.

Grabbing a couple of candles from a kitchen drawer, after I'd opened a bottle of wine, I carried both through to the living room and settled myself by the fire. One of the beauties of the house is its stillness. Nothing stirred but the vibrant flames, and then there were the flames from the candles.

What broke the silence were my quiet sobs. Lifting my glass, I toasted a beautiful friend departed.

'Go, girl,' I said.

*We could never learn to be brave
and patient if there were only joy
in the world.*

HELLEN KELLER

23

Slash, Burn, Poison

Everything felt perfect about that Thursday afternoon. There was a touch of rain, so that I knew I was in Ireland. There had been a bit of sun, to prove that it was August, and the cab I jumped into opposite the Dail was clean. 'Mater Private, please,' I told the driver. 'And can we take Gardiner Street?'

I knew this drill so well. I was heading to the hospital to get my 30th radiation treatment. These last five were called boosters, and that Thursday, with my last radiation booster, I was completing what is jokingly called the slash, burn, and poison stages of breast cancer treatment. That's surgery, chemotherapy and radiation therapy. My eyebrows and eyelashes were growing back, as was my hair, although I kept shaving it.

I couldn't believe that this phase of my treatment was about to come to an end and I meant it when I told the radiographers that I was going to miss them. The Mater Private isn't just a hospital, it's a small community of which I was a part as an out-patient reporting in five days a week.

Having driven me before, the driver remembered me before I did him, but as soon as I saw a bit of his face in his rear-view mirror and studied the back of his head for a second, I realised that he was the big guy with the short-cropped salt-and-pepper hair who'd told me about his wife falling.

I rarely pass up the chance to talk to taxi drivers. They all have such different stories and angles on life that they've been part of my Irish education. One treat of my thirty days of radiation treatment was that for each visit but three, I took a taxi to the hospital. Twice I walked and once I was dropped off by a friend. And though Ted Doyle had offered to give me a lift that Thursday, I wanted to make that journey my usual one. It was also more than enough that he had brought me my mail from the Bel Air as well as the large navy-blue Ralph Lauren box that Fidelma thought I might be needing.

I didn't know that I needed it myself until I opened it, and how she knew on that particular day is beyond me. But then, Fidelma Freeman is probably a bit of a psychic.

It was far too chic a box to have a brown string tied around it, so I removed it and then the lid with the simple gold lettering that said Ralph Lauren. Perhaps Fidelma, or maybe her loyal assistant, Carmel, who works at the Bel Air, had tied the box to keep things from falling out. It held quite an assortment.

When I was renting Number 3 of the Bel Air chalets, the box had arrived with a white angora poncho that was my Christmas present from Mick. I assumed that he never selected these tokens himself and always thanked whichever assistant was working for him. In this case, it was Stephanie, who had impeccable taste, and the poncho was really appropriate for me with my single breast. But it was the box that I got the most use from, because it fitted so well under the coffee table.

I made it the safe place for what I called my cancer things. As I sat in the back of the taxi, checking what was still in the box, I discovered little bits of my cancer trip that I'd forgotten had been part of it. Like pills that I never took and prescriptions that I never had filled, because they were for ills that I never got, including nausea, tummy aches and fatigue. Then there was a pill checklist, which I had held so dear that first week home from the hospital, when I couldn't remember what to take when from the bag of medication that I'd been given.

An article that I'd forgotten I'd clipped from the *Irish Times* reporting on the vomiting disease at St Vincent's was beneath a catalogue from specialists in mastectomy wear. It seemed perverse that page after page featured pictures of sexy young girls modelling their perfect breasts in pretty bras and bathing suits. Next, I thumbed through the pamphlet about lymph edema, the swelling in the arm which I dreaded, and I was just about to read a page when the driver asked, 'How are you feeling?'

'Fabulous,' I said. 'It's my last day for treatment. Well, not quite my last day, but sort of. Anyhow, the main thing's I'm alive.'

'You got the right attitude,' he said. 'They say that's what it's all about.'

'How many times have I heard that?' I was thinking, and I didn't believe a word of it.

I started skimming the pamphlet about lymph edema, which had a good illustration of the lymphatic system. But I get dizzy reading in moving vehicles and was putting it away just as the driver asked again how I was feeling.

Maybe he'd forgotten that he'd already asked.

'Great!' I said this time. 'And, hey, could you turn left up

247

there, like we did the last time? Sorry, I'm not as chatty as I was before, but I just have to look in this box.'

In addition to the box I had a black cloth bag that looked like it was for either shopping or hiking. It was full of cards and tubes of pure cocoa butter for each of the eight radiographers who'd been treating me in teams since mid-July and two of my radiologists, the medical doctors who specialised in radiology.

The only blemish on that Thursday afternoon was that Dr Anne Gribben was having a week's break. Although she'd already had a couple of tubes of my pure cocoa butter, which isn't available in Ireland, Anne deserved a better goodbye present, because she'd given me my initial examination for radiation treatment and, having measured the site of my operation, had also given me my markings, meaning that she marked where the radiation beams were to go.

Until I tried reading a *Radio Oncology* magazine, which I borrowed from Dr Maher, my main radiologist, I didn't know how much pure science was involved in radiology. I popped in each day like I was dropping by for a facial, and in truth it was just as pleasant. There was always pop music playing, and the technicians in their 20s had lives outside of work that I enjoyed hearing about. One treated me to stories about her visit to the Galway races, from another I heard about her brother, who played Gaelic football for Ireland. I teased the guys about their hair gel and the girls about their passion for shoes, and, initially, when the treatments started, I tried to wear an interesting pair each day for the remarks it bred while I was lying on my back getting measured up to be zapped. But they were also well informed and there was no question that I asked about my treatment that they weren't equipped to answer. Since they each warned me that I'd grow progressively more tired as the number of treatments mounted, I tried to grab a nap every day, and my energy wasn't so depleted that I couldn't write or take part in filming for the documentary when it was necessary.

What I did notice was that I had to exercise my arm religiously to retain the ability to stretch it to the full, and it was another reminder that while so much fuss was made of the mastectomy, it was the removal of my lymph glands that caused most of my discomfort.

The five booster treatments that Dr Maher wanted me to have at the end of my general radiation treatment only took five minutes, and it seemed that no sooner than I got my top off and laid down, the young radiographers were saying, 'Thanks, Marsha, all done.'

'That's it?'

'Yep.'

And I'd hand them my little appointment book to get the following day's appointment.

On the way to my last treatment, the taxi driver asked the question I'd heard so often.

'Does it hurt?' he said, as we drove past children playing in Mountjoy Square.

'Not at all,' I said, still rooting through my Ralph Lauren box. 'You don't feel a thing. Just hear this weird noise for about 50 seconds that sounds like something from a sci-fi movie. Then the radiographers come in and reposition the big radiation machine to zap you from another angle, before they slip out of the room again. I guess the rays are radioactive.' I didn't mention that this happened while I was lying on my back, naked from the waist up. Nor did I say that some people's skin gets a bit charred, but having moisturised mine several times through the day and night with cocoa butter, the skin on the right side of my neck and chest had darkened but not cracked. Again, I had dared to do what I was sure would work for me – pure, unadulterated cocoa butter being a slightly greasy substance that my grandmother considered as essential in the medicine cabinet as aspirins, iodine and her beloved blue bottle of Bromo Seltzer.

Patients completing treatments, be it the surgery, the chemo or the radiation, often send a thank-you card or bring a big box of chocolates to be shared amongst the staff that have been treating them. When I asked a radiographer what might be more appreciated than another box of chocolates, she said, 'The kind of junk that kids like to eat.' So as well as cards and cocoa butter for each of them, that's what I brought: a gift bag filled with hard-boiled sweets, various types of mints and caramels and those little white gummy milk bottles that I used to love to eat myself. Along with the soft-drinks machine in the waiting room, it was a disgrace that these dire sugary morsels were supposed to be a gift for a team concerned with cancer and health.

When I walked into reception, carrying my Ralph Lauren box, the black bag and sweets, I couldn't believe that I'd come to this stage of my cancer journey.

The previous day I'd had to be phoned, because I forgot that I had a 2 p.m. Herceptin treatment in the day oncology ward. When I answered my mobile phone and heard the Australian accent of a nurse in the oncology and radiation department, I jumped to the defensive, saying, 'I've just this second looked at my little radiotherapy appointments booklet, and I'm not due until 4 p.m.'

'It's your Herceptin treatment I'm ringing about.'

I barely let her finish the sentence, 'Oh, Christ! Oh, for fuck sake! Selena, I'm so sorry. Can you believe it, I'm sitting here writing and haven't even got dressed yet!' It was three o'clock, and the Herceptin treatment is so expensive that I was meant to ring to confirm I was coming first thing in the morning so they could order it from the hospital's pharmacy. I said, 'I was thinking that I only had radiation today!'

'Not to worry. Can you get here?' She assumed that I was out at the Bel Air, which is an hour from town.

'I'm in Dublin. I'll throw on my things and be there in 20 minutes, assuming I can find a cab.' It was yet another kindness from my friends Kathy Gilfillan and Paul McGuinness that while I was getting daily radiation treatments, they gave me the keys to their Dublin house so I could use it while they were out on U2's world tour.

Herceptin therapy has been described as the biggest advance in breast cancer treatment of the last quarter century. Herceptin is an antibody which targets cancer cells and also stimulates the body's natural defence mechanisms to help destroy the cancer cells. Treatment involves a course of injections taken every three weeks for up to a year and each course costs around £20,000. I saw it as a vital part of my treatment and couldn't believe I had forgotten the appointment.

That Wednesday, when I was rushing through the double doors of the oncology department for my late Herceptin treatment, I apologised to Dr Ameer Behbehani, who is Dr McCaffrey's Kuwaiti registrar.

Dr Ameer said, 'Not to worry. It's a good sign that you forgot.'

'Why?'

'It means that you're moving on, and that this is not the most important thing to you,' he said, indicating the day oncology room where I had spent so many hours getting my chemotherapy. My four Adriamycin treatments, administered every three weeks, followed by the four Taxol treatments every second week, had taken from the end of January until the end of June. It had been a bit longer than expected due to a couple of minor interruptions, like the pneumonia I was diagnosed with as April got under way.

I'd had some really good times in that room, thanks to my cancer buddy John Caffrey, whom I'd first met when we were getting our scans and both wearing black silk pyjamas. Twice when we were in getting treatment at the same time, me in a bed and him in a leather easy chair in the next cubicle, we pulled back the curtain that separated us and treated the session like a happy day trip, enjoying our chat and the lunch and tea that was served.

'What're you gonna have?' I asked him, after Marie O'Donnell from the catering staff reeled off the day's lunch menu and recommended the fish and the banoffi pie. 'You goin' for that, Caff?'

'Sounds good to me,' he said.

'Me too, Marie.'

'All right,' she smiled. Always in a good mood she was, like the nurses rushing about.

After Caff and I finished that lunch and had a little sleep, we woke to Marie O'Donnell tempting us to tea and coffee. We nearly got into trouble, we giggled so much, even making jokes about the fact that maybe we were dying.

When our days eventually got switched, so that I came for treatment on Wednesday and Caff was on Friday, I swore that it was because we'd been so rowdy. But who wouldn't have enjoyed our tasty lunch? And he would have had the Pope laughing with his story about the matchmakers who preside over Lisdoonvarna's traditional match-making festival. Caff tries to go every year for all the fun.

'And what, somebody picks out a bride for you? Come on. Surely that doesn't still happen?'

'Course it does,' he said. 'The custom is centuries old and takes place after the harvest when farmers come to find a bride.'

Once, when I asked Caff if he had any negative feelings about cancer, he thought about it a moment and said, 'Why me?'

Since statistics say that one in three will be hit by this disease, my answer is 'Somebody had to get it, why not us?'

The Beginning

Sure, I left out some important bits, because there were enough to fill two volumes, but as far as I was concerned I had included the most salient aspects of my cancer adventure and there was no more to tell. My editor, Ailsa Bathgate, disagreed. She said, 'But I want to know what happened.'

'How can you say that when you've just read the whole thing?'

We were in Edinburgh, smack in the centre of town, in this beautiful apartment I'd rented on Dublin Street, with its kitchen window overlooking the National Portrait Gallery. It's a block from Mainstream, my publisher, and I'd flown in two days earlier from Dublin to incorporate all the editorial changes that Ailsa wanted before sending my manuscript off to the printers. We were rushing to get the book out in conjunction with my cancer journey documentary, which ITV had decided to call *Beating Breast Cancer*. Since it was airing in two weeks, on 26 September, Ailsa and I and the production team were working against the clock, and the last thing I needed to hear was that she'd finished reading my manuscript and needed more information.

She said, 'The reader will want to know what happened after all that. How you feel now that it's all over . . .'

'But it's not really over. I've got ten more months of those intravenous Herceptin treatments that I'll be receiving every three weeks. And next week, Dr McCaffrey has scheduled me for a major examination to check that there's no cancer . . . Apart from the balls of my feet being incredibly sore, which is a side effect from the last four chemo treatments of Taxol, I've got no physical complaints. I just have to keep exercising my right arm, trying to stretch it as much as possible. It's prone to stiffness due to the surgery and radiation treatment. But otherwise I feel fine. Who wouldn't?'

'A lot of people,' laughed Ailsa.

'But it comes down to that saying, "Is the glass half full or is it half empty?" I'm incapable of seeing it as half empty.' And pointing to a bottle of water that I'd been drinking, I said, 'Look. I'm not seeing the emptiness; I'm seeing the fullness. I'm seeing what remains. And that's the same with me. I don't now look at my naked body and see a breast missing. I see how much positive healing has taken place in that area where the breast had been. I'm looking at how supple I've managed to keep the skin that might have been charred by the 30 hits of chemotherapy had I not rubbed the area with cocoa butter about two dozen times a day. I'm seeing that the flesh along the cut looks much less mangled than it did six months ago, when MRSA had it looking like a bad burn. On the down side, I'm sorry that the steroids have put an extra 30 pounds on me, but I know that with some determined effort I can get my weight down and my muscle tone back.'

Ailsa was looking at me with that look she has when she's

dissatisfied with an answer that I've given her but isn't admitting it yet. I use the word 'yet', because she'll eventually get around to it in the most inoffensive way that she can think of. She's got brown hair and a high forehead that is full of a good brain, and before we met, something about her voice on the phone had me thinking that she was one of those sensible Scottish redheads. She's way prettier and softer looking than she sounds. But behind her feminine guile is that sensible school marm that she sounds like on the phone. So after I'd given her that spiel about my scar, she waited for a good few seconds before she poked me with that piece of guilt about leaving my reader dissatisfied.

Editors always use this when they want to get their way, because what writer wants their reader to close their book feeling dissatisfied?

'But the reader will want to know how you feel in yourself,' Ailsa said.

'I swear to God, I feel great. Cancer's been a wonderful experience for me. One of the best experiences that I've had. Even if I'm dying, I've had a very good time, made some wonderful new friends like Caff and Dee Dee, and a nun named Patrice that there wasn't time to write about. And I've been more productive during these past nine and a half months since Arnie diagnosed cancer than I've ever been in as short a time. Apart from managing to take care of myself, cook and clean and fight my corner with the medics and disease, I've started and finished writing my cancer book plus dealt with goodness knows how many cameramen and sound technicians and people, including Eamon O'Connor and Stuart Prebble, who were working on the documentary. How many planes have I been on to tend the house and garden in France, and the place is still standing and so am I.'

Ailsa said, 'Do you think that a good part of your experience is the way that people appreciate you more and let you know it? Friends rally when they think that they're going to lose you. You know, under normal circumstances most people don't tell you how much they value you, but . . .'

Before she could finish the sentence, I was thinking about how my cancer had improved my relationship with Karis. The incredible closeness that we'd shared when we were a single-parent family had drifted with us being 6,000 miles apart and her having her own nuclear family. She had texted me only the night before my meeting with Ailsa to say that Jonathan was finishing on a movie and they were thinking that they'd come visit with the kids. What more could I want? I texted back, 'Hooray! Can't wait.'

My family, not just Karis but also my brother, Dennis, and sister, Pamala, and her adult daughter, Stephanie, have not only made it a habit to ring me regularly from California, but they also now ring each other. That didn't happen before I got cancer. After our mother, Ikey, died from lung cancer in September of '99, Pam and Dennis spoke on Christmas and their birthdays. My cancer has made them confidants. They can commiserate about me flying too often and doing too much.

I forgot to tell them that I was in Edinburgh because I didn't know that I was coming myself until the day before I caught the plane. I'm not used to keeping anybody informed of my movements, and working on my Jimi book got me in the habit of jumping on a plane or a train at a moment's notice if the chance to interview someone came up. Say as it had with Keith Richards when I heard I had cancer.

I told Ailsa, 'You may think I'm crazy, but I don't give a shit about not having a breast, and as far as losing my hair's concerned, it's trying to grow back and I'm shaving it every day because I love not having to deal with it. I've been totally liberated by my baldness.'

Yet the biggest thing that has happened during this journey has been emotional. Falling in love in cyberspace brought the sound of violins into my life. Todd's symphony of sorrow made me forget myself. We haven't danced nature's wild dance this time around, but our momentary fling 40 years ago was about that. The memory of being together in Berkeley when we were hardly more than children is something that time can't take from us, just as it shall never be able to take these past seven months we've shared through words.

He recently wrote that I had been more there for him than he for me. Did it matter? What mattered is how cancer led me to fully experience that love which is not of the flesh but of the spirit. Like I wrote to him the first day we began e-mailing, cancer's been good to me. And even if it takes me out of here, suppose, just suppose, the documentary and the book help others to cope, whether it's a woman with breast cancer, her husband or a friend, that will mean that, on top of everything, I've contributed something towards the common weal. And isn't that what we're here for, to make life a little better for others?

Hints for Happiness

Once when I was sitting in the oncology reception a bit broke, bald, single breasted and maybe dying, another out- patient whom I saw regularly there asked me why I always seemed so happy. I had to think for a minute and said that it was probably due to a lot of things that I accept and some other things I do most days. Here's a shortlist:

Life's not easy . . .
Shit floats up on everybody's shore when least expected. Accept this, and when it happens, it's less of a shock and a knock.

Being grateful . . .
Whatever's working could stop working. Be it your thumb, eardrum or rectum. By starting the day by taking one minute to go through my body, thinking about how good it is that what's working is working, I start gratefully.

Don't turn on the radio, the TV or look at a newspaper . . .
There will be nothing about me personally in this media that I don't know. To start the day with a load of bad news over

which I have no control makes me feel powerless. I can't do a fucking thing about a plane that crashed in Russia while I was asleep in London, so why do I need to know? And that DJ talking like he's about to miss his bus or like he's rushing to a breakfast party that I'm missing, he'll usurp my interest in what's happening in my house and neighbourhood that I can change. And those TV personalities who had a professional make-up artist do their face and hair before stepping before the camera could make me feel ugly. Our media is always selling us something, and I don't buy into it.

Lighting a candle for someone . . .

That little flame reminds me of my good wish for a friend, living or dead.

Sing . . .

OK, so you're tone deaf and have a lousy voice. Does it matter? What matters is that we can make music for free. Our voice is part of our natural self. Whether it was 'Mary Had a Little Lamb' or the national anthem, we sang as kids and should continue to. You'll be shocked by how happy it makes you to sing a little every day.

Look at an inspiring quote . . .

I find a quote that fires my spirit and stick it up where I can spot it easily. 'Don't give up, your miracle is on the way' is one that keeps me hanging on until the next hour or tomorrow or next week.

Pretend you're not afraid . . .

Everywhere there's potential danger, be it in the streets or countryside, in your bank account, your mind, body and life. Act brave and you'll be brave.

Grow something . . .

The world has grown too impatient for its own good and growing anything involves soil, and time and care.

Doing the dishes . . .

You have a dishwasher? All the more reason to stick your hands in some water and wash the plate that you ate off. It's time consuming. That's the point. It forces you to engage in something unpleasant that takes time. And, yeah, you can always sing, while you do it!

Find a quiet spot . . .

There's a quiet place to stop and rest for a few minutes even in the heart of Manhattan. Find your spot. Go there a couple of times a week. Sit. Be quiet.

Write a letter to a friend . . .

Snail mail's wonderful. To write a letter and post it gives me a sense of achievement. Even a badly written one with sloppy handwriting is a joy. For the price of a stamp, I can send a little joy.

Look your best . . .

For no one's sake but my own, I have days when I pull myself together the very best I can. It's like dressing up on Sunday used to be.

Live adventurously . . .

Even if it's discovering that you have cancer, all life's an adventure. To treat it as such makes the day-to-day challenge of dealing with it a bit of fun.

Respect death . . .

Everyone dies. Death isn't treachery. It's a mystery. Along with birth, it's one of life's bookends.

Be gentle with yourself. Be kind . . .

And remember what Henry Wordsworth Longfellow said:

Not in the clamour of the crowded street,
not in the shouts and plaudits of the throng.
But in ourselves are triumph and defeat.

Thank You

Aileen Blackwell
Aileen Flavin
Ailsa Bathgate
Aisling Gleeson
Alan Dunn
Alan Gilsenan
Alan McShane
Alexandra McGuinness
Ameer Behbehani
Andrea Luria
Anne Counihan
Anne Gribben
Arnie Hill
Barbara O'Reilly Hyland
Bassam Alghanim
Becky Pickard
Berna O'Donovan
Bill Campbell

Undefeated

Bill Cross
Boscoe Hogan
Brian Godbold
Carla van der Vecht
Cillian Guidera
Clare Reihill
Clodagh Duff
Cormac Keane
Cynthia Webb
Deborah McNaughton
Declan Conlon
Declan Heeney
Delia Roche Kelly
Dennis Hunt
Derek Speirs
Doctor Assaf
Dominic Faccini
Eamon O'Connor
Edna Robinson
Edna Tromans
Edward Tobin
Eithne Mulherne
Elisca Coelho
Emily Bland
Enda McDermott
Enid Graddis
Fabienne Toback
Frances Tomelty
Francesca Moseby
Gael Gahagan
Gerry Callanan
Graeme Blaikie

Thank You

Hans van der Vecht
Hassan Shuman
Howard Doyle
Ib Jorgensen
Inez Hunt Hennix
Isabel Prime
Jack Meehan
Jeremy Toback
Jerry Hall
Joan Duff
Joan O'Donnell
John Caffrey
John Callanan
John Ladner
John Lonergan
John McCaffrey
Johnny Price
Jonathan Caffrey
Judy Lewis
Julia Kennedy
June Housden
Karis Jagger
Kathy Gilfillan
Keith Richards
Kevin Singleton
Kirsty Wilson
Macken Pharmacy, Black Rock
Madeleine Kingsley
Magella Doyle
Maggie Duff
Mainstream
Marie Doyle

267

Undefeated

Marilyn Prebble
Marina Fonesca
Mary Counihan
Mary Elizabeth Mastroantonio
Marte Kaplan
Martina Smith
Mary Counihan
Mary Travers
Max McGuinness
Mazie Rane Watson
Mick Jagger
Michael Maher
Pamala Farve
Pat O'Connor
Patricia Van der Leun
Paul McGuinness
Paul Nicholas
Peter MacKenzie
Ramon Gurillo
Richard Arbach
Richard Graddis
Robert O'Byrne
Robert van der Vecht
Sarah Doyle
Sharon Atherton
Sheila Scott Wilkinson
Sherry Daly
Simon Albury
Steph Lawrence
Stephanie Desverney
Steve Lovi
Stuart Prebble

Thank You

Susan Hunter
Susan Sandon
Ted Doyle
Thelma Palena
Tim Counihan
Tom Hickey
Tim Curry
Tony Garnett
Ulla Allen
Vincent Howieson
Will Nash
Zachary Watson